A Storytellers Guide

to a

GRACE-FILLED

Life

70 Plus Stories & Reflections of God's Grace

Tony Agnesi

ISBN-13: 978-0692965665 (Virtu Press)

ISBN-10: 0692965661

PRESS

DEDICATION

This book is dedicated to Nico and Luca, my wonderful grandsons:

Faith is a gift from God handed down from generation to generation. May these stories of faith and family help to guide you in your journey through life and bring you the joy of a grace-filled life. That is my eternal prayer.

Love,

Grandpa

> Report it to your children. Have your children report it to their children, and their children to the next generation. — (Joel 1:3, NAB)

RoseMary,

God Bless you!

Tony

TABLE OF CONTENTS

Chapter 3- God's Grace at the Holidays

Chapter 4- God's Grace in Daily Life

Chapter 5- God's Grace in Prayer

INTRODUCTION

I'm a storyteller. While that's not a huge revelation, I just discovered that fact in the past few years. I have always been a storyteller. I come from a long line of storytellers. My grandmother was a storyteller, so was my mom, and it just makes sense that I am too.

Over a career that spans nearly 50 years, I have always used storytelling as a means to motivate, lead, and manage in business. I found it easier to explain things by telling a story that made my point. It always got the message across in a memorable way. What I have found over the years is that former students, employees, and friends will recall a particular story that meant a great deal to them. Often they will tell me that my stories have changed their lives or at least the way they approach a situation.

Often, I've been told that I should write down some of my stories, to document them in a way that they might be helpful to others.

While I have always been a storyteller I have never fashioned myself as a writer. I remember vividly in my freshman year of college being told by an English professor that I write at a 6th grade level!

Her words deeply affected me and kept my storytelling strictly spoken until four years ago. I decided sixth grade level or not, I was going to sit down and share stories with whoever would read them. That's when my blog *Finding God's Grace* began. Since then, I have been writing a new story every week for over four years.

About three months into my writing, I asked a friend from church, a former English professor, to read some of my stories. She really enjoyed reading them, so I couldn't help but ask her, "What grade level do you think I write at?"

"That's easy," she said, "About seventh grade."

"Well," I thought, "at least I'm up a grade!"

This book is a digest of 73 of these stories, categorized by subject matter and all telling of God's amazing grace, lessons learned and reflections intended to resonate with you and cause you to recall the stories of God's presence in your own life.

The recalling and retelling of our encounters with God, those stories and events that change our lives, are the backbone of our faith. They weave the fabric of our faith. Your story is an important part of *the* story. Never be afraid to share your encounters with God. You might just change someone's life.

In these pages, I'll share mine.

Chapter 1:

GOD'S GRACE IN FAMILY

Lord, Teach Me to be Faithful

When people think of Italian-Americans they automatically assume "Catholic." And, usually that's true. So when I tell friends that my Father was an Italian Methodist, they look at me in dazed confusion.

When my dad and mom married, my dad agreed that his children would be raised in my mom's Catholic faith, an agreement that he took seriously.

Each week, he would drive Mom, my sister and me to 8:30 a.m. Mass at St. Francis. While we were at Mass, he would drive across town to St. Dominic's and pick up the Dominican nuns who taught our Sunday school class (Confraternity of Christian Doctrine) after Mass.

He would then wait in the car during class, reading the Sunday newspaper or listening to the Italian Show on local AM radio.

After class, he would take the sisters back to St. Dominic's, drop my sister and me home, and drive to his Methodist church for services at 11 a.m.!

That was his routine, every Sunday, without fail for over 12 years! You see, when Dad made a promise; he kept it.

Over the years, I often wondered why he just didn't go to Mass with the rest of the family. In my teen years, I prayed for his conversion, but, somehow, I was never able to broach the subject with him. What I did know is that he was faithful not only to the promise he made to raise us in the Catholic faith, but also to his own upbringing.

In my collections of Bibles and Christian books, none are more valuable to me than the small Bible Dad carried with him during World War II, (a gift to him from his church for his handyman work) and two Methodist Hymnals, one Dad's and the other my Grandfather's.

One of the greatest lessons Dad taught me was faithfulness. He was faithful to God, faithful to his wife and family, and faithful to his friends. He was a good man, a good Christian, and truth be told, a better Catholic than most.

Reflections: *Who taught you the lesson of faithfulness? How important is being faithful to a good relationship? Have you ever been unfaithful to another?*

Church, My Mom Made Me Go!

Hear, O Israel! The Lord is our God, the Lord alone! Therefore, you shall love the Lord, your God, with all your heart, and with all your soul, and with all your strength. Take to heart these words which I enjoin on you today. Drill them into your children. Speak of them at home and abroad, whether you are busy or at rest. — (Deuteronomy 6:4-7, NAB)

Faith was the center of my Mom's life. Everything revolved around the church; Mass, confession, holy days, and Christmas and Easter. She was a tireless worker, and with a few of her like-minded friends, she kept everything at our tiny little church shiny and clean. The vestments and altar cloths were pressed to perfection. Candle holders were polished to a brilliant shine.

My Mom was also a stickler for attending Mass and confession. As a kid, I never got away with not attending Sunday Mass and confession on Saturday mornings. Because the church was so small, I served Mass as an altar boy until I was in my early 20's including weekday Masses, holy days, and lots of weddings and funerals.

It wasn't really my choice, Mom *made* me go!

As I look back now, it was the faith that my mother passed on to me that has sustained me in tough times; colon cancer, hepatitis C, pneumonia, and family tragedies.

Her faith became the beautiful faith of my wedding and the baptism of my sons. It became the centerpiece of birthdays, holidays, beautiful Christmas and Easter family gatherings. All centered in the faith my mother *forced* on me.

Thank you Mom! I didn't realize it then, but now I see that my faith in Jesus Christ and his Holy Catholic Church was the greatest gift I have ever received. Sometimes the greatest gifts we receive are the ones that we fail to appreciate until much later in life. Thanks, Mom, for making me go.

Reflections: *How do you share the faith with your children? Do you think that your faith has rubbed off on your children? How important is passing along your faith to your children? What one thing can you do to help your children see how important faith is in your life?*

Evening in Paris

A childhood memory of my mom is *Evening in Paris* perfume. It was touted in the 1950's as "the fragrance more women wear than any other in the world!" When she and Dad went out for the evening, she would bend down to kiss me goodbye, and the sweet smell of *Evening in Paris* would fill my nostrils until they returned. I have always associated the scent of that perfume with my mom and happy times.

Each Mother's Day, my sister and I were given a small amount of money to purchase something for my mom. That was easy! I had my dad drive me to the local Grey Drug Store, where I would scan the cosmetics counter until I spotted that cobalt blue bottle. Aaah...*Evening in Paris*!

Even though she knew in advance, she always was thrilled to get a bottle of *Evening in Paris*.

Years later, my Mom lay dying in her bedroom, suffering the pain of cancer. This was before today's pain management drugs. Members of our family would take turns spending some time with her. We would hold hands; pray the rosary, and talk, when she was able.

On her bedroom dresser were two things that meant a lot to her. One was her Infant Jesus of Prague statue that we got her for Christmas one year. It was a statue with different color vestments, changed by liturgical season. My sister kept the Infant supplied with many options, with her gift money from Dad.

Next to the Infant was her bottle of *Evening in Paris*, prominently displayed. What was in actuality an inexpensive drug store perfume stood as though it was the most expensive perfume in the world.

I recently read that *Evening in Paris* perfume was back on the shelves, although reformulated. It's expensive now. The cobalt blue bottles from the 1940's and 50's are worth many times more as antiques that the perfume cost back then.

Contact your mother today. Tell her how much you love her, and remember it is not how much a gift costs, but the lifetime of memories that might result. It just might be her *Evening in Paris!*

Reflections: *Do you have a found memory of your mother? What one word describes your mother? If you are a Mom, how would you like to be remembered?*

Happiness is Wanting What You Have

> The world tells us to seek success, power, and money; God tells us to seek humility, service and love. — (Pope Francis, 2013)

My wife, Diane, has a simple philosophy that is displayed on a small plaque on our windowsill: Happiness is wanting what you have!

That's it, pretty simple! Appreciating what we already have is the cornerstone of contentment. It is gratitude in its purest form. Pope Francis said, "The world tells us that success, power, and money should be our goals. Advertising points us to the latest 'must have' possessions and reinforces that we are not successful, if we don't have them."

Some people line up like lemmings to get the latest iPhone when their current still works fine because they worry about what people think if they don't have the latest model? Others proclaim that even though they have an 80-inch television, they can't live without the 94-inch screen. Perhaps you've been asked about your car, "You mean you don't drive a BMW or Mercedes or Porsche? How can you possibly be happy?"

We are so busy wanting, that we fail to appreciate what we already have.

My wife chooses to count the blessings God has given her, rather than dwell on those things she doesn't have. She doesn't covet any of her friend's possessions. She is happy for them. Happy that God has blessed them. In her gratitude, she finds contentment—humble, loving contentment.

I find that the happiest people I know are the ones who center their lives on Jesus. They realize that the philosophy of "he who dies with the most toys wins," is not the way to heaven.

Try this experiment. The next time you pray the rosary, mention something that you are grateful for on each bead. I guarantee that you won't run out of things to be grateful for. Or make a list of things that you have that you are grateful for. You won't have any problems filling the entire page.

I promise that when you finish, you will feel happy, humble, grateful, and more content. Then, try to remember that feeling. Happiness is not found in acquiring more "stuff" but rather the "attitude of gratitude," derived from wanting what you already have, and counting those things as blessings from God.

What are you grateful for today?

Reflection: *What are you grateful for today? Do you sometimes covet what others have instead of treasuring what you have? Do you ever reflect on those that have very little?*

It's Friday, and I Have a Date!

Mom was a very spiritual woman. One of her favorite devotions was to attend Mass on the nine first Friday's of the month, in honor of the Sacred Heart of Jesus. It's an old devotion and the promises have wonderful graces attached. Often, I would attend Mass with her on these days.

Several years ago, my wife, and I were discussing this devotion and decided to give it a try. We faithfully made the first Fridays of the month for a couple of years, and then one day she said, "Why don't we just go to Mass every Friday?"

"You know, that's a great idea!" I replied. "And after Mass, we can go to breakfast together. It would be like a date every Friday morning."

That was over a decade ago, and every Friday, without fail, we go to Mass and then to breakfast. It has become our weekly daytime date!

In this busy world, where it is difficult for married couples to find the time for meaningful one-on-one conversation, our weekly date has become a blessing. We have discussed every imaginable topic and have never run out of things to talk about. The tradition has brought us closer together.

Whether it's Mass and breakfast, or some other combination of spiritual and shared time together, it is important to make it an unbreakable pact.

When our sons were little, we would go to vigil Mass on Saturday evenings, and then go to dinner as a family, which our kids always looked forward to. It didn't have to be an expensive restaurant, just a place where we could all be together and share our lives.

For Diane and me, no matter what problems or challenges the week holds, Friday morning is sacred.

Why not give it a try? Find a time and combination that works for you as a couple or as a family, and make it non-negotiable.

Hey, how bad can it be? Like me, you will always have a Friday date!

Reflections: Is there something you do daily, weekly, or monthly with your spouse that is priority one? Do you and your spouse have a regular date night? How important is it to continue to date your spouse even after many years of marriage?

Daily Mass, You must be Holy!

Holy Communion separates us from sin. The body of Christ we receive in Holy Communion is "given up for us," and the blood we drink "shed for the many for the forgiveness of sins." For this reason the Eucharist cannot unite us to Christ without at the same time cleansing us from past sins and preserving us from future sins: For as often as we eat this bread and drink the cup, we proclaim the death of the Lord. If we proclaim the Lord's death, we proclaim the forgiveness of sins. If, as often as his blood is poured out, it is poured for the forgiveness of sins, I should always receive it, so that it may always forgive my sins. Because I always sin, I should always have a remedy. — (Catechism of

the Catholic Church [hereafter CCC],
(Image Books/Doubleday, 1995),
1393

When people find out that I attend Mass every day, they say something like, "You must be really holy!" They just don't get it.

I usually share an old saying, "Mass is not a sanctuary for saints, it's a hospital for sinners, and I'm in intensive care!" I attend Mass daily because of what it does for me, personally, spiritually, emotionally, and physically. I go to Mass because doing so makes my life better.

Here are a few reasons why I go and what it does for me;

1. It keeps me in an uplifted mood that lasts all day. I'm ready to tackle the problems of the day with Christ by my side. I am energized by God's grace!

2. It keeps me focused on others and not on myself.

3. It gives me the strength to fight the occasions of sin that day. I feed my body every day (as my weight would attest), so why not feed my soul as well?

4. It increases my gratitude for the many blessings that God has heaped on me. Praising God first thing in the morning with prayer and Mass is the most important events on my daily calendar.

5. I am surrounded by others at Mass who are also working out their salvation, and they inspire me to do more. They too, are energized by God's amazing grace.

6. Daily scripture and the brief homily become daily guideposts for the day.

7. My friendship with Jesus is important. I want to spend some time with Him, hang out with Him, talk with Him, joke with Him, laugh with Him and cry with Him, just as I do with my earthly friends.

Not everyone can attend daily Mass. Time famine is one of the biggest problems facing adults today. Jobs, raising kids, and work-related travel is overwhelming. Nevertheless, take some time to recharge your battery with the electricity of God's grace. It's there for the asking, every day, at Mass.

Reflection: *How can I find a way to increase my Mass attendance and reception of the Eucharist? Can I add one day of Mass attendance during the week? Does a church in my area offer a lunchtime or evening Mass*

Time is All We Have

Eight years ago, I had cancer surgery. It was a scary time, but one that I wouldn't trade was what taught me about the value of time.

Most of us live as if we will be around forever. We say, "I don't have time for that" or "I'll start going to church when I am older, right now I just don't have the time." It reminds me of the country song, "Everybody wants to go to heaven, but nobody wants to go now!"

We procrastinate to later. Unfortunately for some of us, there won't be a later. Ultimately, this misuse of time is a denial of death. We just don't realize how precious time really is. I didn't until the thought of that time being shortened hit me before my surgery. I went about my life as if I had all the time in the world.

We really need to focus on what is important, on what is the best use of our time. We need to think about what will bring us the best reward. Time is all we have.

When I see a workaholic friend bemoaning that fact that he has no time, I remind him that I have never met a man on his death bed who said, "I wish I would have spent more time at work!" More time with his wife, family, friends, more time in prayer, serving others, but never more time at work.

Eight years following my surgery, I still feel like I am on borrowed time. Five years is considered a cure. It makes me value every minute. I'm one less rat in the rat race!

Faith, family, and friends—these are what is important. Enjoy every moment.

Reflections: Have you ever lost a young friend or relative? If time is all we have, what are you doing to quit wasting it? Have you ever put off something that you later regretted?

The Winter Coat

> Give and gifts will be given to you, a
> good measure, packed together shaken
> down and overflowing, will be poured
> into your lap. — (Luke 6:38, NAB)

Growing up in a blue collar family, having a new coat for winter was a welcomed gift. That is one of the reasons I remember my Aunt Jay. Each year, she would scrimp and save money from her 90-cent an hour job at the dry cleaners. She would use the money to buy winter coats for my cousins, Diane, Steven, and Susan, and my sister Angie and me. And, believe me; it takes a lot of hot sweaty hours in the laundry to pay for five coats. But she did, and it wasn't until I became an adult that I realized what a sacrifice that was.

My wife, Diane works with the local pregnancy center. Diane was in charge of their Christmas room a few years ago. The center provided coats and winter clothing for the children of their clients. They provided toys and gifts as well.

One day, I read in the paper that a local Penny's outlet was selling coats at a low price. Remembering Aunt Jay, this was my opportunity to pay it forward and provide coats for needy kids. One Saturday morning, Diane and I made our way to the outlet. As advertised, there were nice winter coats in all sizes. I was like a kid in a candy store loading up two shopping carts with coats in a variety of sizes and colors.

Shoppers crowded the store that day and the checkout lines were long. As I maneuvered the carts through the store, a young clerk was opening another checkout. She motioned me toward her checkout. I rushed to make my way and was the first in line at the new checkout. As I moved toward the line, I noticed that the young checkout girl was pregnant and her eyes red from crying.

I smiled and tried to make some small talk when she asked me, "Wow, you have a lot of coats here, where are you taking them?"

"To the Pregnancy Center," I replied. "What is that, she inquired?"

As I explained, her tears returned as she began to tell her story. "I'm pregnant and my parents kicked me out of the house. My boyfriend left and all I have is this part-time job and a room I am renting. I don't know how I will ever support a child, I need everything!

Immediately, Diane jumped in to the conversation, telling her that there was help. She gave her a card with the address and number of the pregnancy center. Diane instructed her to call on Monday and make an appointment.

Not long after that day, she had her baby, a big healthy boy. She got the help she needed from this wonderful organization. She received a crib, layette, blankets, formula, and diapers. In addition, spiritual help from a caring staff and volunteers that were all waiting for her at the pregnancy center.

I realized that our trip to the outlet that day to buy coats was a "God Appointment." Our meeting this beautiful young girl was a gift from God. And the fact that she opened the checkout line for me, made it clear.

She got what she needed for her baby, and as a bonus, a coat for herself that was the right size and color.

I could picture Aunt Jay, snapping her Juicy Fruit chewing gum, and smiling her special smile. She would pause and enjoy only for a moment, because then it would be time to start saving for next year.

Reflections: Was there someone in your life who sacrificed for you? How did it make you feel when you realized how much love was involved? Have you ever been the "angel" for someone?

Enjoy the Mangoes

Can any of you by worrying add a single
moment to your life-span? — (Matthew
6:27, NAB)

When we are given a gift, we often are at a loss for words. "You shouldn't have." "I can't accept this." "I really don't know what to say." The responses go on and on. What if we simply said thank you! That's it, just "Thank You!"

Following my cancer surgery, when I learned that I was cancer-free (eight years now, thank God!) I had a million questions. My wise doctor told me of an old saying in India: *"Aam Khao, ped, kyon ginte ho?"* Loosely translated, it means: Enjoy your mango, and don't worry about what particular tree it comes from.

In other words, God has blessed you with a gift, a cancer-free diagnosis. It isn't important to know every detail of the surgery, it's is only important to enjoy the gift. Too often we get hung up on the details, and forget that it is the gift that's important.

This is what happens when our thoughts are fixed on the future and not the present. We spend so much time worrying about the details, that we forget the gift that is the present. For me, it was worry about the surgery, recovery, my wife, family, and even death. I spent so much time worrying, that I failed to stop and simply thank God, and enjoy the mangos!

To avoid worrying about the future, we must savor and relish the present. Enjoy your surroundings, the people close to you, and the beauty of the day. Live in the moment! Every moment of every day is a gift to be enjoyed, right now. Elizabeth Gilbert, in her bestselling book, *Eat, Pray, Love* tells of a friend who sees a beautiful place and exclaims, "It's so beautiful here, I want to come back some day!" What she fails to realize, is that she is already there! She needs to enjoy the beautiful place *now*. She needs to stop and enjoy the mangoes!

Reflection: What are you going to do to recognize God's gifts and enjoy the mangos? Do you spend time living in the present moment or are you worried about sharing your experiences on social media?

Attentive or Distracted

> Since you cannot do good to all, you are
> to pay special attention to those who, by
> the accidents of time, or place, or
> circumstances, are brought into closer
> connection with you. — (St. Augustine)

Dad, are you listening to me? Honey, we talked about this yesterday, don't you remember? Bob, you said you would pick up the kids after school. They waited for over an hour, why can you do this one simple thing?

Attentiveness has really taken a hit in this fast-paced, time-starved world we live in. There is always something else going on in our minds. Our smart phones are constantly ringing, beeping, and buzzing with the latest call, text message or email. We just can't seem to catch up or catch a break. We miss the present worrying about the past and anticipating the future.

Debbie makes her way through the grocery store with three kids, all under five-years old, in tow. The youngest is in tears, dropping her Pooh Bear over the side of the cart to the floor. The five-year-old wanders off to check out the cookie aisle. Meanwhile, Deb is tethered to her smart phone, planning a party for her sorority sister, while her kids are begging for her attention.

Bill has finally gotten a night off to spend at home with his kids. They are eager to share their stories of soccer games and a cheerleading competition with him. But Bill's mind is a million miles away. He is worried about the big presentation he has to make in the morning. He half listens and later can't remember a thing they shared. The next day during the presentation, Bill feels guilty for not being more mindful of them.

Brad and Sue have been married for two years. Sue can't wait until Brad gets home from work to share the good news about the promotion she got at work. Brad walks in the house, barely acknowledging her, and making no eye contact, grabs a beer from the refrigerator and plops down in his easy chair. Brad's only concern is the rumor that his company might be laying off workers, including him. He misses the opportunity to share in her joy and have her console him in his fears. Brad and Sue are heading for divorce.

> Therefore, we must attend all the more
> to what we have heard, so that we may
> not be carried away. — (Hebrews 2:1
> NAB)

No one would disagree that living in the moment, mindfulness, and being more attentive to the present sounds wonderful, in theory. But doing it is another thing!

How can we be "all-in" for our spouse, kids, friends, and coworkers? How can we put aside the problem from yesterday and be mindful and more attentive to what is happening right now?

Here are a few things we can try;

1. **Remove the distractions**. When you get home from work, remove the smart phone and your car keys from your pocket and put them away. I place my keys on the counter and plug my smart phone into the charger. I consider it a success when I don't touch it again until I leave for work in the morning.

2. **Quit multi-tasking and do one thing at a time.** Many people would say that's impossible, but research indicated that when you are shopping, watching your three kids, and talking on your smart phone, you will do none of the tasks well.

3. **Make eye contact and listen.** Your spouse and kids know when you are paying attention. You stop what you are doing, make eye contact, and listen. Kids want Dad to look them in the eyes and be truly happy for their accomplishments.

4. **Ask questions.** If you are not getting the whole story or are having trouble following, ask questions, get clarifications. If you do this, you won't be in the big presentations wondering what your kids said to you the night before.

5. **Start with their life before yours.** You have things to share as well. But, make a habit of listening to stories from your spouse or children before sharing yours. Be attentive!

Want a balanced, happy, and fulfilling life? Practice attentiveness. Be mindful of what is happening right now, with your spouse, kids, and friends. Try to be more attentive to what the Lord is asking of you. Clear away the distractions and listen. God is speaking to you. Listen!

Reflections: Are you so distracted that you aren't attentive to your family? Does worrying about the past consume your mind? Are you always so anxious about tomorrow that you miss the joy of today? Try putting your cell phone out of reach for two hours every night.

The Myth of Quality Time

> He said to them, "Come away by
> yourselves to a deserted place and rest a
> while." People were coming and going in
> great numbers, and they had no
> opportunity even to eat. — (Mark 6:31,
> NAB)

What is more important, the quality of time with your family or quantity of time? We have spent the last 40 years convincing ourselves that quality time is more important. But is it?

In today's fast-paced culture, business comes first. Two working parents are the norm and finding time is difficult. So, we rationalize that quality trumps quantity. We give lip service to the relationships we have with our spouse and kids. We promise to spend some "quality time" with our kids, but rarely do.

A survey a few years ago said that the average child spends 30 minutes a week with his mom and 15 minutes with his dad, hardly quality or quantity time.

Twenty-five hundred first graders were asked, "What is the one thing you want to have more of?" Their answer was "more time with my mom and dad!" And, it's not the once a year trip to the zoo or amusement park they want, but just time hanging out, being together, being close.

Has the myth of quality time become a self-serving rationalization for not spending time with family? Is it a way of deluding ourselves into shortchanging our children and spouses?

Do you want good kids? Then, spend some time with them. Real parenting takes place when we are together. Real parenting is spontaneous, and opportunities to teach life lessons happen when we are least expecting it. It's something that can't be planned and scheduled on your calendar like

30

any other appointment. You can't say, "I think I'll give my family a little quality time Wednesday from 2 until 3." Sorry, it doesn't work that way.

So, what can we do to have more time with our families, spouses, and kids? How can we give them the time that they deserve? Here are a few ideas to try:

1. **Have dinner together.** In my family everyone agrees that sharing dinner as often as possible, every night if you can, is one of our favorite times. It has become a valuable family tradition. It gives family members a time to talk, share, ask questions, and feel part of something bigger than them. It connects us to each other.

2. **Leave the smart phone at the door.** Like most people, I am tethered to my smart phone all day. But, when I walk into the house at the end of the day, I leave my smart phone at the door. Being connected 24 hours a day makes every call, text, email, and Facebook notification more important than your family. Recently, I saw a guy at a hotel pool vacationing with his family. He was splashing around in the pool with his kids but he was wearing a Bluetooth headset in case some important call came in. Really? Stop it!

3. **Cut out the non-essential activities.** Poker nights, Monday Night Football at the local pub with friends, girls' night out, and that extra Zumba class are great, but don't make them an excuse for not spending more time with the kids. Some nights might be better spent at home playing games, eating pizza, and watching TV as a family. Plan that special date night with your spouse this week, then next week take the same amount of time to plan an activity with your family.

4. **Make some time for prayer.** Grace before meals, a bedtime prayer before lights out, and thanking God for the time we have together binds us as a family and give us a sense of gratitude for our blessings. I have heard many people say that their greatest regret was not spending more time with their spouse and kids.

Time flies, kids grow. In the blink of an eye they will be young adults. Don't miss the opportunities to spend some time together. Remember, there is no real "quality time" unless you have some "quantity time."

Reflections: Do your kids ever ask you for more time? Do you ever use work as an excuse not to spend time with your family? Do you ever just spend some time hanging out with family? If you work eight hours a day and sleep eight hours, how do you spend the remaining eight hours?

Become Like Children

At that time the disciples approached Jesus and said, "Who is the greatest in the kingdom of heaven?" He called a child over, placed it in their midst, and said, "Amen, I say to you, unless you turn and become like children, you will not enter the kingdom of heaven. Whoever humbles himself like this child is the greatest in the kingdom of heaven. And whoever receives one child such as this in my name receives me. — (Matthew 18:1-5, NAB)

This week, we returned home from a trip to California to visit my son, daughter-in-law, and grandson Nico, especially Nico! It was wonderful and I got to spend plenty of time with this sixteen-month-old non-stop energy dynamo.

I'm exhausted, but in a very positive way I have a new appreciation of what it takes for young couples to raise little ones. It seems the older we get, the more we push away the memories of those sleepless nights, never-ending diaper changes, and meals that end up on the floor.

I recalled that just before I left for California, I read the gospel of Matthew that said we need to become like little children to enter the kingdom of heaven. So, what is it that makes children better candidates for heaven? What are the attributes that Jesus is talking about that we need to model?

As I observed Nico over the next few days, it all became much clearer to me. Here are a few things that I observed about little children:

1. **They live in the present.** The most important thing to a child is what they are doing right now. They aren't depressed because of some event of the past or anxious about something they must do tomorrow. They simply aren't concerned about anything except the Legos or puzzle or book right in front of them.
2. **They practice unconditional love.** Children have the ability to be happy no matter what. They can go from crying to giggles in a matter of seconds, completely putting out of their mind the reason they were crying only moments earlier.
3. **They are humble and meek.** Children totally submit to their parents, rely on their parents and trust their parents to be there when danger is near.
4. **They live in simplicity.** Children accept thing as they are; they don't question things or become jealous of others' homes, cars, or income.
5. **They are full of awe.** Children have pure hearts, taking in everything around them with wide-eyed awe. Their first trip to the zoo, playground, or water park is experienced with pure joy.

So, what can we learn from them? What are the things that Jesus is suggesting when he says we must be like one of these children?

Like children, we need to live in the present. We need to understand that living in the past causes depression and living in the future causes anxiety. We must be mindful of the moment and live each day to its fullest.

In doing so, we must practice unconditional love. Our joy often comes from serving others, being there for family and friends, and being less judgmental.

We need to be humble and practice gratitude, kindness, and forgiveness. We need to be grateful for what we have and not spend valuable time being jealous.

We also need to simplify our lives and view the world with the same awe as a child.

Most importantly, we can't do this on our own. We need to have that same humility and total trust for God that our children have for parents and grandparents. It's a wonderful feeling to know that Jesus has our back, if we only submit to his loving touch.

Turn away from self-reliance, away from sin, to a simple, humble, awe-filled, It's amazing what you can learn from a sixteen-month-old child. If we turn loving life, we can prepare ourselves to enter heaven and maybe, like a child, experience heaven on earth.

Reflections: What have you learned about Jesus from your children or grandchildren? How can I become like a child? What must I do differently?

Where there is Love, There is God

> We have come to know and to believe in
> the love God has for us. God is love,
> and whoever remains in love remains in
> God and God in him. — (1 John 4:16,
> NAB)

I am in awe of young parents and their never-ending battles of keeping up in this fast-paced, always-connected world we live in. With soccer practice, gymnastics, diaper bags, and juggling jobs, family life, and their kids' busier-than-ever social schedules, there just isn't much time for God.

These days, life moves at a fever pitch. For those of us a bit older, we long for simpler times, when life just seemed to move more slowly. We had more time for family, friends, and God, but times have really changed!

Many older adults are quick to criticize and ask the question, "Where is God in all of this?" Saint Mother Teresa offers this,

> What you are doing I cannot do, what
> I'm doing you cannot do, but together
> we are doing something beautiful for
> God, and this is the greatness of God's
> love for us. — (Saint Mother Teresa,
> 2012)

Parenthood is a full-time job! As we long for a time when kids just went outside to play until called home, now we spend every waking minute worrying about our kid's safety. While we recall a time when we worked for the same company for 40 years and retired with a gold watch, today's parents worry about the next round of layoffs and whether they can find another job.

We need to give young parents a break! This isn't 1950. They are doing the best they can, and they are doing it with great love.

If God is love, as we read in 1 John 4:16, and we abide in Him, then, where there is love, God is there too! The love and attention that they give their children is proof positive that God is with them!

Here are some hopefully encouraging thoughts for young parents:

1. **God loves us!** Isn't that cool! John reminds us, 'If we love one another, God remains in us, and his love is brought to perfection in us." (1 John 4:12, NAB) The more you love your kids the more you are bringing God's love to perfection.

2. **God abides in us, if we abide in Him.** What does abide mean? In this context it means to stay or remain with Him, as John tells us, "Whoever acknowledges that Jesus is the Son of God, God remains in him and he in God." (1 John 4:15, NAB) It's that simple. If we believe that Jesus is the Son of God, He is with us.

3. **God wants good things for us.** If we truly believe, then we shouldn't fear the future. "There is no fear in love, but perfect love drives out fear because fear has to do with punishment, and so one who fears is not yet perfect in love." (1John 4:18, NAB) Our worries should be replaced with faith that God will see us through tough times, job loss, financial problems, sickness or pain.

4. **God is always there for us.** No matter how busy we are or how frazzled our day has been, we can always call on God for help. We can maintain a constant dialogue with God throughout the day. It's easy and it's the simplest form of prayer.

5. **God knows our sacrifice.** Just getting kids ready for Sunday Mass is a chore. Getting everyone dressed, packing the diaper bag, car seat, a few books to help with distractions, and that bag of Cheerios takes time. Sometimes it feels like it's not worth it. Believe me, it is!

No matter what others might say, I am one older adult that appreciates modern parenthood and the sacrifices parents make. When I see the love couples share with each other and with their children, I know that God is there too! As we sing in the beautiful, old Latin hymn, "Ubi caritas et amor, Deus ibi est." In English, "Where charity and love are, God is there."

Reflections: Do you appreciate the challenges that today's parents' face? Do you think that in today's fast-paced society has made parenting harder than ever? What can we do to help parents of young children cope?

Chapter 2:

GOD'S GRACE IN VIRTUES

Kindness and Truth Shall Meet

> Kindness and truth will meet; justice and
> peace will kiss. Truth will spring from
> the earth; justice will look down from
> heaven. — (Psalm 85:10-11, NAB)

A wise rabbi once said that the world is sustained by three things, justice, truth and peace. When justice is done, truth is served and peace is achieved.

In Catholic social teaching, we understand that non-violence denotes peace with justice; that we should be peaceful, truthful, and loving in our relationships, especially with those who don't share our opinions.

Martin Luther King stood on these non-violent tenants as well. He understood that peace cannot be achieved by conflict, rioting, and unrest. It can only be achieved by a constant call for justice, stating of the truth, and softening the hearts with kindness. When we approach social justice with kindness and truth, justice and peace will follow.

Mahatma Gandhi said that, 'Non-violence is not a garment to be put on and off at will. Its seat is in the heart, and it must be an inseparable part of our being." (Farnham, D., 2014)

Sadly, that's not what we see on the evening news today. In our country we see rioting, looting, and violence. We see young men losing their lives with excessive reactions, policemen killed while sitting in their patrol cars, and people over-reacting, with so-called leaders fueling the fire of violence.

And across the world we see beheading, young school girls kidnapped, and men and women being martyred for their faith.

The wise rabbi would teach that this is not the way to peace. Catholic social teaching would argue that we should peacefully get people together to find a solution, one of the greatest leaders of social justice in the 20th century, Martin Luther King, would beg us to stop the violence, and Gandhi would tell us that "An eye for an eye will only make the whole world blind."

What has happened since the death of Doctor King to undo the work he gave his life for? Where are the leaders, especially religious leaders, who will continue the legacy of non-violent protest?

Our country needs leadership, not neat thirty-second sound bites on the news. We need people who understand the process to initiate the conversation, do the hard work, usually behind the scenes, and move our country to a better understanding of the truth.

The world needs leadership, not savagery that is disguised as faith.

What we don't need are leaders with their own political agendas, lining their pockets while their followers are rioting in the streets and much of the world is unsafe.

Where is the next Gandhi, Mandela, Kennedy, or King? Where are the leaders that can show us a better way? Most of the world religions teach the same principle of kindness and truth, justice and peace. We need leadership that can get this done. I hope and pray that these leaders will emerge.

Until then, I'll keep praying for peace.

Reflections: What are you doing to support peace? Where do we find the leaders to show us the way to peace? What are you doing to promote social justice?

Open to God's Grace

For by grace you have been saved
through faith, and this is not from you; it
is the gift of God. — (Ephesians 2:8,
NAB)

There is an old saying, "If you want light to come into your life, then you need to stand where it is shining." For many people, suffering hard times make them withdraw and keep their feelings inside. They move further and further away from the light of God's grace and into the darkness of their own solitude.

Have you ever built a fire on a cold winter night? If you want to get warm, you move closer to the fire, right? We all know that the closer we stand to the flame, the greater the warmth.

The same is true for God's grace.

If we want to be wrapped in God's grace then we must move toward Him. We must move into His light and be warmed by the fire of His amazing grace!

There are many times in our lives when we feel alienated from God, stuck in our own fears, worry, and anxiety. We retreat into ourselves, away from the light, away from the warmth of the fire of God's love, mercy, and grace.

In times like these, we need to move toward God, recalling the places and times that we felt close to our Savior and going there.

Where can we start?

1. **Try gratitude.** When we are so self-absorbed in the problems of the day, being grateful for the blessings we have starts us on the

path to grace. Grace and Gratitude have the same Latin root, Gratis. Whenever you find yourself feeling like nothing is going right, stop for a moment and think of your blessings. Being grateful for what you have will help you with the grace necessary to deal with your situation.

2. **Try Forgiveness.** Countless people say that going to the sacrament of confession and receiving absolution flooded them with God's grace. Confessing our sins and seeking forgiveness has a powerful healing effect.

3. **Try reaching out to a friend.** Do you have a friend that is going through tough times? They may have had a recent surgery, lost a loved one, are having relationship problems, or recently lost a job. Reach out with a phone call, a card, or better yet, a visit. Helping your friend will help you through your own tough times.

4. **Try serving others.** Taking the focus off our problems and helping others with even greater challenges not only takes our minds off our problems, but triggers our own sense of gratefulness. Visit an elderly relative in a nursing home or volunteer at a homeless shelter food pantry. Serving others will renew a sense of the Lord's presence in your life, and trigger a sense of gratefulness.

5. **Try rediscovering.** Reflect on the places where you have encountered God's grace. Ask yourself, "Where have I felt the Lord's presence in the past?"

It could be a church, a favorite spot in the park, favorite bike path, or favorite easy chair.

It could be a memory of a favorite day, a wedding, the birth of a child, an award you received, or a time that in helping someone you felt the overwhelming rush of God's grace.

Pope Francis tells us, "Grace is not part of consciousness; it is the amount of light in our souls, not knowledge nor reason." (2013)

Do you want to increase the amount of light in your life? Then, stand where it is shining, in the loving arms of our Savior. Do you want to feel the glow of God's mercy? Then move closer to Him, close enough to be bathed in the warmth of His grace.

Reflections: How can I move closer to the light and God's grace? How does gratitude and forgiveness bring God's grace? How can I overcome suffering and become closer to our Lord?

The Power of a Smile

A glad heart lights up the face, but an anguished heart breaks the spirit. —
(Proverbs 15:13, NAB)

Last night, I was looking through some pictures from our recent visit to California, a trip to see our ten-month-old grandson, Nico. I noticed that in every picture he had a big, slobbery smile. And, as I looked at the pictures, I couldn't help but smile too!

I recalled that I smiled the entire time I was in California, and Nico's smile had a lot to do with that! The pictures make the smiles return.

Smiles are contagious. No matter how you are feeling at the time, seeing someone smile (especially babies) will make you smile as well.

When we are feeling happy, we smile. But, smiles work both ways. When we see someone smiling, we smile, and even if just for a moment we feel happy.

Smiles are very powerful. Research indicates that people who smile a lot live longer and look better. Portman Healthcare's research says that in addition to living longer, smiles help reduce pain, strengthens our immune system, reduces stress, and makes us more successful.

Some will say that they have nothing to smile about. Their problems are too big and complicated to crack a smile. They live with a dull sense of despair. But you can help.

Your smile can be the spark that helps turn thing around. Your smile can help cut through the despair.

Years ago, while working in my first job, I asked a successful, older fellow worker why he was so successful with women. He wasn't that good looking, he was bald and overweight, but he was always smiling and surrounded by pretty women.

He said, "Smile at the pretty girls and it will make you feel good. Smile at the not so pretty girls and it make them feel good. So, smile at all the girls."

Today, years later, I can extend his thoughts to include everyone. "Smile at everyone you meet and it will make you happy. They will smile back because smiling is contagious and it will make you happy. So, smile at everyone!"

Want to live longer, have a better marriage, be more successful, reduce pain and stress, and strengthen your immune system? Then, start with a smile.

Say cheese!

Reflections: *Do you agree that smiles are powerful? Have you ever had your mood changed by the smile of a child? What can we learn about smiling that can help us in our everyday lives?*

Lord, Help Me to Forgive

> But I say to you, love your enemies, and
> pray for those who persecute you, that
> you may be children of your heavenly
> Father, for he makes his sun rise on the
> bad and the good, and causes rain to fall
> on the just and the unjust. — (Matthew
> 5:44-45, NAB)

There is a story of two holocaust survivors who meet when they are in their late eighties, and they are discussing their time together in a German concentration camp.

"I am still angry after all these years. I can *never* forgive what they did to me," said the first survivor. "What about you?"

"Oh, I have long forgiven them," said the second in reply.

Shocked, the first man asked in an angry voice, "How could you forgive what they did? I will *never* forgive them!"

"Then, you are *still* their prisoner," he humbly answered.

Many people hold on to anger and resentment about things that have happened in their lives years ago, incidents that they just can't get past.

Being cheated or abandoned by a spouse, family member, friend, or coworker can have a lasting effect our inner-peace.

Over and over, people will play back the incident, and the hurt, the anger, and the resentment is eating away at them.

They don't understand that *Anger is a banquet, and they are the entrée.*

The person that hurt you isn't losing any sleep or giving it any thought. As a matter of fact, they probably don't think about it at all! But it is eating at you!

The only road to peace is forgiveness. We must forgive them, and put the incident behind us, for our own peace of mind. Like the holocaust survivor in the story, by not forgiving, he is still, after all these years, held captive.

What if the person who hurt me isn't sorry? Remember, we need to pardon before we are asked or even if we are never asked.

Do you remember the old saying, "To err is human, to forgive divine."
 It's true. We as humans make terrible mistakes, decisions, and do hurtful things to each other; especially to the people we love. But to forgive is divine, and we are *not* divine. Only God has the divine power to forgive, and we can only make the decision to accept God's grace to forgive.

Give forgiveness a try. What have you got to lose? Decide to accept God's grace to forgive those who have hurt us in the past. Then, thank Jesus for the miracle of forgiveness.

Reflections: Do you have trouble forgiving? Do you hold on to anger and sometimes can't remember why? Does the story of the holocaust survivors help you to understand the reason you need to forgive?

In the Blink of an Eye

A thousand years in your eyes are merely
a yesterday, before a watch passes in the
night, you have brought them to an end.
They disappear like sleep at dawn; they
are like grass that dies. It sprouts green
in the morning; by evening it is dry and
withered. — (Psalm 90:4-6, NAB)

Time flies is an expression we hear all the time. And it's true. Often, when people talk about their jobs they will say, "This is not what I wanted to do with my life, but I took this job, and in the blink of an eye, I was with the company for ten years. And, then twenty years passed. The next thing I knew, they were giving me a gold watch at retirement."

It's sad that they never got to do the things they really wanted to do, the job they dreamed of as a kid. Time just passed them by so quickly.

So much of life happens in the blink of an eye.

In the blink of an eye, we fall in love. One minute your heart is your own, and in the blink of an eye, it belongs to someone else.

In the blink of an eye, a baby is born, and our hearts and lives, as parents, are changed forever.

In the blink of an eye, we get the diagnosis that we have cancer. And our life is immediately altered and our future is uncertain.

We fight with a loved one—a parent, spouse or adult child—and in the blink of an eye, a traffic accident takes them from us and we never get the opportunity to say we are sorry.

Life changes so quickly. Within the context of eternity, our time on earth is just a blink of God's eye.

What can we do to savor our time and squeeze every second out of the time we have?

First, we must live in the moment. Joy and happiness are in the *now*, and we must slow down to appreciate it. We spend so much time planning for tomorrow that we miss the joy of today.

Next, we need to let go of the past. We miss the joy of today, if our minds are in the past.

We need to practice gratitude. We need to appreciate the things we have and resist the "got to haves" we are bombarded with every day. "Let your life be free from love of money but be content with what you have, for he has said, I will never forsake you or abandon you". (Hebrews 13:5, NAB)

Finally, never pass up an opportunity to say "I love you" or "I'm sorry." You may never get another opportunity to do so. For some, these are hard words to say, but in saying them often, we can live without regrets. Remember, life happens in the blink of an eye. Enjoy today, tomorrow will come soon enough.

Reflection: *Have you blinked your eyes and a year has gone by or even a decade? What can we do to savor the time we have together? Do you try to live in the moment? How difficult do you find it?*

Be Kind

[And] be kind to one another,
compassionate, forgiving one another as
God has forgiven you in Christ. —
(Ephesians 4:32, NAB)

As I drove home on a beautiful Friday afternoon, I passed an elder care facility and noticed a woman in her motorized wheelchair smiling as she made her way down the sidewalk enjoying the day.

A car was coming in the other direction, and as it got closer to the woman, I could hear a volley of derogatory comments from a car full of teenaged boys. The things they yelled at this poor woman were unbelievable! She was just enjoying the day.

Who would do that? Why do people continue to put other people down? Does it make these teens feel better about their hollow lives by putting down an elderly woman in a wheelchair? Because people are different, why do we feel we need to berate them? "To belittle, you have to be little." - (Kahlil Gibran, the Prophet)

The loneliest people are the kindest. The saddest people are the brightest. The most damaged people are the wisest. All because they do not wish to see anyone else suffer the way they do.

As I drove on, I began to think about my own judgmental behavior. Unwittingly, I find myself judging others.

The antidote is *kindness*.

Our job is not to judge who is and who isn't worthy of our kindness, our job is to be kind unconditionally, without fail, even when it is difficult to do so.

Here are some things we can do to be kinder and less judgmental and to live our lives in a new, compassionate and respectful way:

1.   **Be open-minded.** People come in different sizes, colors, and cultures. Plato said, "Be kind, for everyone you meet is fighting a hard battle." We don't know what they are battling. Be kind.
2.   **Appreciate People for who they are.** We all have unique qualities; celebrate the things that make us different.
3.   **Smile, say hello, and thank you.** Simple things like a warm greeting, a big smile, and a thank you can make someone's day.
4.   **Say a kind word to a stranger.** You will forget tomorrow the kind words you said today, but the recipient may cherish them for a lifetime.
5.   **Give people hope.** Encouragement has lasting value. Challenge people to keep their vision alive.

This week, make an effort to be kind. If we are conscious of our interactions, we can be successful. Let's try it for a week and see if kindness makes a difference. Make it a way of life. Maybe it will rub off on others, like those teenagers in the car berating the woman in the wheelchair. We can only hope.

Reflection: *Has there ever been a time when you were unkind and later regretted it? Why do you think people belittle others? Does it make them feel better about themselves?*

I'd Rather Be Happy than Right

Stop judging and you will not be judged.
Stop condemning and you will not be
condemned. Forgive and you will be
forgiven. — (Luke 6-3, NAB)

There is a song on the radio that makes me smile every time I hear it. It's called, "I'd Rather Be Happy than Right." Years ago, I was talking to a friend about his marital problems. He just couldn't get past the feeling that he was right and his wife was wrong in a variety of problem areas.

I asked him the simple question, "Do you want to be right or do you want to be happy?"

"Well, both!" he answered.

"That would be ideal, but people have different points of view. What is right to you might not be right to her," I offered.

The question of happy or right is one that I have struggled with. I found that when confronted with a problem, argument, or disagreement, if I ask this question, often I will choose to bite my tongue and opt for happy.

What do I have to gain from being right, besides a temporary ego boost? Shouldn't I be thinking about the long term? Isn't that what relationships are about?

In the self-justification world, the most dangerous word we can use is "but". I agree, **but**, you said. You're right, **but** you are a jerk. I could forgive you, **but**, it has happened too many times.

If we can let go of righteous indignation and forget the "buts," then we have an opportunity to find happiness.

Today, our culture is fixated on right and wrong. Everything is black or white, Republican vs. Democrat, Liberal vs. Conservative, Pro-Life vs. Pro Aborts, gay marriage vs. traditional marriage; there seems to be no place for a middle ground or compromise. There is no discussion, no one can make a point, and no one *ever* changes their mind.

I am not saying that we have to give up or compromise our position on issues. But, we have to realize that not everyone thinks alike. We judge people, and often reject them, before we have had a chance to hear their opinion.

When it comes down to choosing between right and happy, from now on, I choose happy!

Reflection: Was there ever a time that you wanted to be right so badly that you regretted your actions? Have you ever made the choice to not argue and choose happiness instead?

To Be Fully Alive

The Glory of God is man fully alive. –
(St. Irenaeus)

Have you ever felt fully alive? I'm not talking about just having a pulse, but a time when you really felt alive.

For some it might be the moment they spoke their wedding vows. For another, the sight of their new born baby a few seconds after birth might bring that feeling. Or, the first time we see the Grand Canyon, the Swiss Alps, St. Peter's Square or other breathtaking sights.

It can be the first time we skydive, speed down a ski slope, score a touchdown, hit a home run, or make a hole in one.

Time stops, just for a moment. Everything seems like it is happening in slow motion, and we are totally in the moment. It feels great to be fully alive!

Being fully alive isn't just about happy times. Sometimes, the feeling of being fully alive comes from pain. The death of a loved one, that cancer diagnosis, the job loss, divorce, or other life-changing experiences, temper us like steel and make us appreciate the life we have. As we look back on these times, we realize that hard times help us to become stronger. We become more understanding, and helpful people. We learn gratitude, kindness, forgiveness, and we want to serve others.

We learn about courage when we face danger or poverty when we are hungry. We gain strength through pushing ourselves through our comfort zones. We learn about sorrow through loss, thriving through striving.

Our Lord, Jesus experienced these same feelings. He knew hunger, danger, sorrow, despair, confusion, and pain.

Remember the pain and suffering of Good Friday, gives way to the joy of the resurrection at Easter.

Many people sleepwalk through life, living just to survive, trying to be comfortable, continually searching for who they are, but are unwilling to be the person they were truly meant to be by stepping out of their comfort zone.

We have got to be uncomfortable to be fully alive. In our pain, we must depend on God to guide us, not to take away the pain, but to make us aware that in suffering through it, trusting completely in Him, we can experience the joy and beauty of life, fully alive.

That life comes through service to others. We can build on the pain we have felt, and focus it on helping those who are experiencing the same problems.

A volunteer at the local hunger center was once hungry.

A man offering a blanket and boots to a homeless man on the street was once on the streets himself.

A woman who visits a cancer patient at the hospital is a cancer survivor.

Jesus reminds us in Mark 8:35, "For whoever wishes to save his life will lose it, but whoever loses his life for my sake and that of the gospel will save it." (NAB)In addition, Pope Benedict XVI, per Spe Salvi tells us "the one who has hope lives differently; the one who hopes has been granted the gift of a new life." (2007)

If you are not serving, you simply exist. Whenever I meet someone who is fixated on their problems, I tell them, "You need a ministry." You need to take the pain you have experienced and use it for the glory of God. I promise you that if you do, you will experience the beauty and joy of someone who has hope, of someone granted the gift of a new life, a life that is fully alive!

Reflection: *Name one time when you felt fully alive? Was it a happy time or a sad one? Do you feel that we can be truly alive in times of sickness, job loss, or marital difficulties?*

The Value of a Good Hug

> And people were bringing children to
> him that he might touch them, but the
> disciples rebuked them. When Jesus saw
> this he became indignant and said to
> them, "Let the children come to me; do
> not prevent them, for the kingdom of
> God belongs to such as these. Amen, I
> say to you, whoever does not accept the
> kingdom of God like a child will not
> enter it." Then he embraced them and
> blessed them, placing his hands on them.
> — (Matthew 10:13-16, NAB)

I admit it—I'm a hugger. Maybe it's because I'm Italian or because I came
from a family of huggers, or perhaps it's because hugging just makes me
feel good.

I am an equal opportunity hugger. I hug old people and kids, women and
men, dogs and cats, family, friends, and even my enemies. I always have
and probably always will.

There is a lot of scientific evidence that hugging has many therapeutic
values. Hugging boosts oxytocin levels, helping relieve loneliness and
isolation. It increases happiness by increasing serotonin levels, and
strengthens the immune system.

Hugs make us feel important, wanted, and loved. Who can resist the hugs
of a child or grandchild burying themselves in your arms?

There are many references in the Bible about greeting others with a holy
kiss or hug. Jesus was a hugger too, especially with children.

A hug is more powerful than a thousand words! This is especially true when a loved one receives bad health news or in consoling a friend at a funeral.

Did you ever have the feeling that God was hugging you? It happens in a fleeting moment, when our thoughts turn to him and we realize that God is with us to comfort us, to bring joy to our lives and to give us His assurance that things will be alright. "God Hugs" are what some folks call them.

A rainbow on your wedding day, a certain song that comes on the radio at a special moment, something we hear, see, or read, All provide little hugs from God. It can be a phone call from a friend that we haven't seen in years or a card or letter from someone letting you know they care.

It's time to get busy. Let's not let another day go by without getting our daily hugs. If you grew up in a family that didn't hug, it might be difficult at first. But you'll get better with practice!

People tell me all the time that I'm a good hugger. I should be! I've had a lifetime of practice!

Have you gotten your hugs today?

Reflection: Are you a hugger? What are the benefits you feel from a good hug? Was hugging something your family did? If not, are you becoming a hugger?

The Value of a Lost Soul

> I tell you, in just the same way there will
> be more joy in heaven over one sinner
> who repents than over ninety-nine
> righteous people who have no need of
> repentance. — (Luke 15:7, NAB)

As the female inmates entered the classroom, I noticed that one of the inmates was pregnant. She seemed close to her delivery date. As the service began, I had a feeling that we should offer prayer for her and her unborn baby.

When I asked if we could pray for her and her baby, her eyes began to tear up.

She said, "No one has ever asked me that before, no one has ever prayed for me."

As we spoke softly, she told of how she was always told that she was worthless, that she was useless, and no one cared if she were dead or alive. I could see that she wasn't suffering from LOW self-esteem, but NO self-esteem!

It reminded me of something a good friend once shared. The value of a lost object doesn't lessen just because it is lost. A lost twenty-dollar bill is still worth twenty dollars. Its maker determines its value, not its situation.

The same is true for a lost soul, it still has great value, because its Maker, God, establishes its value, and God doesn't make worthless or useless souls!

In Luke, chapter 15, Jesus shares three parables about lost things and their value. In all three—the lost sheep, the lost coin, and the lost son—he ends each story with his concern for the lost and God's love for a repentant sinner. Jesus values lost souls.

This poor girl had been beaten down for so long that she didn't realize she had great value in God's eyes. Like the shepherd who left the ninety-nine to go after the lost one, we should all join in rejoicing that this lost sheep has been found.

I asked the other inmates and ministry team to lay hands on this inmate and pray for her and her baby. As we began to pray, several of the other inmates prayed aloud for her and for a healthy baby. They prayed that she would get her life together and become the person and mother she was meant to be.

She was in tears. She realized that she was loved, and the concern for her and her baby was genuine. For the first time, someone said she was special, a loving person, and would be a great mother. She wasn't worthless or useless. People cared for her.

Most people have never witnessed inmates praying for another inmate. These prayers are very powerful, offered through the power of the Holy Spirit.

> First of all, then, I ask that supplications, prayers, petitions, and thanksgivings be offered for everyone, for kings and for all in authority, that we may lead a quiet and tranquil life in all devotion and dignity. This is good and pleasing to God our savior, who wills everyone to be saved and to come to knowledge of the truth. — (1 Timothy 2:1-4, NAB)

These may be lost souls *now*, but they still have great value. In 1 Timothy 2:1-4, we learn that Jesus wills everyone to be saved, even those in prison.

Before we begin to judge others, please remember the story of the twenty-dollar bill. Its value is not diminished because it is lost. And when a lost soul is found, there will be much rejoicing in heaven.

Let's judge less and love more. Jesus, make me an instrument of your peace!

Reflection: Have you ever encountered a person with low self-esteem? What can you do to explain to her how important she is in God's eyes?

Living Your Resume or Eulogy?

I conducted a time management seminar for around 40 people. Whenever I make this presentation, I ask the group "Why do you want to manage your time better?" The responses are varied but most revolve around time famine. They want to get more done, make more money or get a better job.

How about managing our time so that we might devote it to things that are really important?

"Are you living your eulogy or your résumé?" I'll ask.

Usually, there are few confused faces because it is a question that many have never been asked.

A recent Huffington Post article talked about redefining success, beyond power and money to include well-being, wisdom, and our ability to wonder and to give, as part of the equation. They call it the Third Metric.

When we remember someone who died, we rarely talk about their money and power achievements. We talk about the quality of their character, what they believed, how they treated others or their strong faith.

We don't recall their number of Facebook friends, the number of times they reviewed the sales figures, or that they never miss a reality show. We remember things like "Joe was a good husband, father, and friend," or "Mary cared about the poor, less fortunate, the sick, and the aged."

In managing our time, we must differentiate between things that are important and things that are urgent. Things like e-mail, texting, smart phones, Facebook, and Twitter are all made to seem important because their immediacy creates a false sense of urgency.

Their urgency doesn't make them important! As a matter of fact, they are the greatest time wasters!

Are smart phone more important that some quality time with your kids? Is being connected with work is more important than being connected with your wife and children? Teens will text their friends hundreds of times a day, instead of getting on their bicycles and spending some time together.

What would happen if we talked to a fellow worker face-to-face instead of texting them? What would happen if we took half the time we spend on Facebook and visited someone in the hospital, Grandma at the nursing home, or served food at a local shelter?

We would be living our eulogy instead of our resume! We would be defining our success by the Third Metric of well-being, wisdom, and our ability to wonder and to give back.

Motivational speakers often speak of the goal of becoming "the best version of yourself" that you can. Isn't that what our Lord is asking of us? To do that, we must realize that the best version of ourselves isn't how quickly we can respond to a text message, or how many e-mail's we get each day, or by the number of our Facebook friends. It is how we use our gifts for the glory of God.

Take the eulogy test. How would you like your life to be described at your funeral? It is not too late to shift gears and make your life matter!

We have the choice of making a living, or we can design a life. We can discover this by asking the question, "What gives meaning to my life?"

That answer will reveal the best, most authentic version of you. Live that and you'll be living your eulogy instead of your resume.

Reflection: *If you were to die today, how would you like your life to be described at your funeral?*

Blessed, I'm Blessed!

Early in my career, I worked with a salesman named Ace. He was the top salesman in the company and took great pride in winning every sales contest the company would offer. Often, he would take me with him on sales calls and not only were we a successful team, but we had fun too!

One of the things I remember about Ace was his answer to the daily question, "Ace, how are you?"

"Blessed," he would say enthusiastically, "Blessed."

I use to think that was a strange answer. After all, everyone else would respond with, "fine," "O.K.," " good," "alright," or some other nondescript answer. But blessed? No one ever said blessed!

Not only did it seem strange, but what did he mean by blessed? The dictionary has several meanings for the word. As an adjective, the word blessed means bringing happiness, pleasure, or contentment. Another is:

characterized by happiness or good fortune. Still another: bringing great happiness or good fortune.

In the gospel of Matthew 5:3-10, at the beginning of the "Sermon on the Mount," Jesus (in almost poetic language) tells us who is blessed;

> Blessed are the poor in spirit, for theirs is
> the kingdom of heaven.
> Blessed are they who mourn, for they
> will be comforted.
> Blessed are the meek, for they will inherit
> the land.
> Blessed are they who hunger and thirst
> for righteousness, for they will be
> satisfied.
> Blessed are the merciful, for they will be
> shown mercy.
> Blessed are the clean of heart, for they
> will see God.
> Blessed are the peacemakers, for they
> will be called children of God.
> Blessed are they who are persecuted for
> the sake of righteousness, for theirs is
> the kingdom of heaven. — (NAB)

Wow! You've got to be in pretty good company when you think of the beatitudes. Yet isn't that what we all should be striving for, to be blessed?

When I think of all the good fortune, happiness, and contentment that the Lord has given me, I feel blessed. Blessed in so many ways!

Maybe getting older has some effect on things, but as I get older, I am more grateful, and thankful for a forgiving and understanding God. Thankful, that God accepts me as I am, with all my faults and flaws. I'm grateful, that he continues to bless me with good health, happiness, a loving wife, great kids, and loyal friends.

Reflection: *If someone asked, "How are you?" Would you answer "blessed"? Do you feel blessed? What do you think of my friend Ace's answer?*

A Quiet Ego

> With all humility and gentleness, with
> patience, bearing with one another
> through love, striving to preserve the
> unity of the spirit through the bond of
> peace. — (Ephesians 4:2-3, NAB)

What ever happened to humility? In the past century, it has been replaced with the "looking out for number one" mentality. Americans have become so self-centered, so self-absorbed that they rarely see beyond their own needs.

Walk through your local book store and you will see hundreds of self-help books, with the overwhelming majority of them so centered on self that humility and gentleness, patience and other virtues are left behind.

A study by Pelin Kesebir at the University of Wisconsin-Madison took a look at the books written between 1901 and 2000 and the results are startling. (610-623)

In the last century, there has been a 74 percent decline in the use of virtuous words in all writing. Words like honesty, compassion, and patience are slowly being removed from our writing.

The words humble and humility are down over 43 percent in that period.

If Tennyson is correct and humility is truly the mother of all virtues, where does that leave us as a society, and what can we, as Christians, do about it?

In the past couple of decades, psychologists and social scientists have sought some middle ground. How do we balance our ego with a humble regard for others? What has emerged is the "quiet ego." It's perfectly normal to have a heathy sense of self. It can be one of our greatest strengths. But, it can also be our greatest enemy!

So, where does that leave humility? Can we have a healthy ego and still be humble? Can we find the balance?

They answer is yes! The bible tells us that there are real benefits to being humble. Here are a few:

Humility brings wisdom. Too much self-centered thinking brings an unhealthy sense of pride. Americans love boastful athletes and celebrities, only to attack them when they fall. Humility is the prerequisite for wisdom.

Humility brings God's mercy. As we become more successful, holding on to our humility will keep us closer to our Lord. We realize that everything we have is a gift, and our talents and hard work are also from God. Staying humble in success opens us to God's grace and mercy.

Humility brings social benefits. Humble people are less prejudiced, more helpful, have more self-control and form better relationships. They are better learners, make higher grades, and perform at a higher level at their jobs.

Sounds good, right? So how do we quiet our egos and find that balance? Here are a few thoughts:

1. **Put God first!** There is nothing wrong with a good sense of self but always remember that all that we have and do is ultimately a gift from God.

2. **Be aware of others around us.** Sometimes we get so hung up on our own day-to-day problems that we fail to see or acknowledge our family, friends, and co-workers who could use a helping hand, a strong shoulder to cry on, or someone that will listen to their story.

3. **Prayer and meditation.** Spend some time each day in prayer asking God to calm our ego and make us more aware of others in our lives. I love the Litany of Humility and pray it often.

If humility is the mother of all virtues, then, a quiet ego might just be the key to leading a better life. Maybe, one by one, we can change the narrative of the 21st century from a decline in virtues to a more virtuous, joyful, and wisdom-filled life in Christ.

Reflections: What can you do to quiet your ego? How can we be helpful to others and still maintain a healthy ego? What can we do to remain humble?

In All Things Give Thanks

I read an article recently that said the words *thanks, thanksgiving or give thanks* are used in the bible 162 times. The word *thanks* alone, 73 times and *thanksgiving* 25 times. I guess that means the bible views ***giving thanks*** as an important element of Christianity.

Unfortunately, we seem to live in a society of want! Gratitude has left secular society to the extent that we are raising a self-absorbed, entitlement generation.

It's not until something bad happens—an illness, disease, the death of a loved one, a disaster, flood, tsunami, or wild fire—that it shocks us into understanding just how good we have it. The richest 300 people in the world have more wealth than the 3 billion poorest. Even the poorest of Americans have more than 80 percent of the world. We all have reason to give thanks.

In the past few weeks, several of my friends have had bad health news; a brain tumor, renal failure, a cancer reoccurrence, and a sudden death of a loved one. In each instance, the persons affected spoke words of gratitude. They were thankful that their problem wasn't as bad as the person in the next hospital bed. They were grateful that the issue was discovered early and that some of the best doctors in the country were available to help. They were grateful, for family and friends who rallied around them in their time of need. And, they were grateful, to a loving and forgiving God for a chance to beat the odds.

Why don't more people get it? Why does something have to happen to get our attention? Is gratitude simply a cute photo slide that we "like" on a Facebook post and never give another thought? Is it just sappy sentimentality?

Or is it a way of life? Should we, as the Bible says, "give thanks in everything!"

> In all circumstances give thanks, for this
> is the will of God for you in Christ Jesus.
> — (1Thessalonians 5:18, NAB)

St. Rose of Lima, in her beautiful writings, speaks of the grace that comes to those who are afflicted with suffering. Suffering is the true stairway to paradise, through the cross and resurrection of our Lord, Jesus Christ. As a cancer survivor, I can attest to that! I am a better person today for having experienced it.

As St. Rose wrote, Our Lord and Savior lifted up his voice and said with incomparable majesty: "Let all men know that grace comes after tribulation. Let them know that without the burden of afflictions it is impossible to reach the height of grace. Let them know that the gifts of grace increase as the struggles increase. Let men take care not to stray and be deceived. This is the only true stairway to paradise, and without the cross they can find no road to climb to heaven."

As you read this, offer up some thanks to God for all that you have. Not for what you need, but those things you already have been blessed with.

Lord, thank you for this day, and thank you for everything that you have blessed me with. Make me a good steward of these many blessings and to share my good fortunes with those in need.

Reflection: *Has there been a trying time in your life that God's grace helped you get through? Do you agree with St. Rose that grace flows to the afflicted and hurting?*

Growing Older is a Blessing

The just shall flourish like the palm tree,
shall grow like a cedar of Lebanon.
Planted in the house of the LORD, they
shall flourish in the courts of our God.
They shall bear fruit even in old age,
always vigorous and sturdy, as they
proclaim: "The LORD is just; our rock,
in whom there is no wrong. — (Psalms
92:13-16, NAB)

A few weeks ago at our Wednesday night men's prayer group, we were discussing New Year's resolutions. I made the comment that every year, as I grown a little older, my resolutions have less to do with job and money and more to do with being a better person.

That's when Dick Hills chimed in. "Growing old is a blessing!" Dick exclaimed. "There is a lot of grace that comes from getting older."

He's right! As we get older, the responsibilities of raising children, making a living, making mortgage payments, and many other things, all decrease, and our desire to have a right relationship with God increases.

We finally have the time to devote to prayer, service to others, and growing in our faith. We have a lifetime of memories that St. Augustine referred to as a "vast court" or a "great receptacle".

> The elderly have a rich storehouse of memories, and inner landscape to explore: times lost in idleness, opportunities well used, a fulfilling career, children grown up and suffering gone through with dignity and courage. — (St. Augustine of Hippo, *Confessions* (Book X)

Viktor Frankl, the Nazi death camp survivor, in his amazing book *Man's Search for Meaning* said:

> There is no reason to pity old people. Instead, young people should envy them. They have realities in the past— "the potentialities they have actualized, the meanings they have fulfilled, the values they have realized – and nothing and nobody can ever remove these assets from the past." – (Victor Frankl, 2000)

Some of the things we discussed that night were:

As we get older, we are more grateful! It is true, as we get older; we realize that life is a gift to be cherished. Some people don't get that gift of time. Our lives are filled with friends that never got the chance to grow old, and we are grateful that we have been blessed.

We grow spiritually! As we get closer to God, we put away some of our old ways and take on a new, more authentic version of ourselves. As the Bible says:

> Put away the old self of your former way of life, corrupted through deceitful desires, and be renewed in the spirit of your minds, and put on the new self, created in God's way in righteousness and holiness of truth. Therefore, putting away falsehood, speak the truth, each one to his neighbor, for we are members one of another. — (Ephesians 4:22-25, NAB)

We have the time to pray for others! One of my favorite things at our Wednesday night prayer group is to pray for others. We start by making a list of all the people we need to pray for and then do it.

> First of all, then, I ask that supplications, prayers, petitions, and thanksgivings be offered for everyone. — (1 Timothy 2:1, NAB)

We have time for ministry! Often older people are the volunteers at the food pantries, homeless shelters, and pregnancy centers. They are active in the ministries of their church, taking up the roles of lectors, communion ministers, choir, and many others.

My buddy Dick was right, growing old is a blessing. I am sure he would agree with Viktor Frankl that young people should envy us!

"Hi-ho, Silver! Away!"

> [But] take care not to perform righteous deeds in order that people may see them; otherwise, you will have no recompense from your heavenly Father. When you give alms, do not blow a trumpet before you, as the hypocrites do in the synagogues and in the streets to win the praise of others. Amen, I say to you, they have received their reward. But when you give alms, do not let your left hand know what your right is doing, so that your almsgiving may be secret. And your Father who sees in secret will repay you.
> — (Matthew 6:1-4, NAB)

One of my favorite childhood characters was The Lone Ranger. I watched with anticipation each week as the masked man and his faithful companion Tonto fought to right some wrong in the Wild West, only to leave town before anyone could thank them.

That was my favorite part of the show, and every show ended the same way. The Lone Ranger wasn't interested in accolades, trophies, or banquets in his honor. He was only interested in fighting for law and order in the Wild West. When he fired his gun, he never aimed to kill, but rather to always bring the bandit in with the least amount of force necessary. Not to mention, silver bullets were very expensive!

When the writers of the show developed the characters, they purposely wrote a creed that the Lone Ranger and Tonto took very seriously. Even the television actors, wanting to be good role models for children in the 1950s, took their positions seriously and tried to live their lives accordingly.

Superman, Zorro, and other fictional characters in the 1950's followed this same code. Star athletes back then credited their teammates, coaches, fans, anyone but themselves for their success. They were humble in their success and lived their lives by a strict code of conduct.

What has happened since then? Now, not a week goes by that we don't have some awards show on television, honoring people for simply doing something. The Lone Ranger did it without accolades. Celebrities donate money to charity in return for getting their name on a building or project. And athletes, instead of thanking their teammates, thump their chest with their very own victory dance of, "it was all me!"

The powerful impact of these old fictional characters still resonates with me, even today.

Forget about applause, honors, or awards. Do great things simply because it's the right thing to do!

Doing the right thing—moral codes, ethics, almsgiving—are all tenants of what it is to be a good Christian, a follower of Christ. When Jesus performed a miracle, he asked those involved to tell no one. He never stayed around long enough for a banquet in his honor.

Christ asks that of us, simply to do things because they are the right thing to do. Help people in need, when no one is watching. Give money to a street beggar, or a family member in a bind, or a charity that does great work, not for the praise, but because the cause is right and just.

I can see it now, as clearly as when I was a kid. "Who was that masked man?" In a loud, clear voice, in front of my twenty one-inch RCA, black and white television, I would reply, "That was The Lone Ranger!"

Reflection: *What can we learn from the code of conduct of the old 1950's superheroes like The Lone Ranger?*

Fishermen and Fishers of Men

> As he was walking by the Sea of Galilee, he saw two brothers, Simon who is called Peter, and his brother Andrew, casting a net into the sea; they were fishermen. He said to them, "Come after me, and I will make you fishers of men." At once they left their nets and followed him. He walked along from there and saw two other brothers, James, the son of Zebedee, and his brother John. They were in a boat, with their father Zebedee, mending their nets. He called them, and immediately they left their boat and their father and followed him. — (Matthew 4:18-2, NAB)

One of my passions is bass fishing. I'll drop almost anything for an opportunity to spend some time on a lake or pond. I find that fishing not only relaxes me but teaches me patience, as well. (One of my core sins is a lack of patience.)

Sometimes, when I am fishing alone, I think of the apostles, and why Jesus chose so many fishermen to evangelize, and why he has chosen me to do the same?

I finally got it! I realized that Jesus picked fishermen because fishing for fish and fishing for men require some of the same skills and techniques. To be good at fishing, you've got to know the habitat, depth of the water, and the type of fish that you are going to catch. It takes patience, and perseverance. Here are a few of the rules of fishing that can also be applied to evangelization.

1. It is how you wiggle the bait. Some days you have to fish very slowly, jiggling the bait off the bottom and letting it drift back down. Other times you have to fish quickly. Every fisherman has his favorite retrieval style, like two twitches and a count of three, or three straight twitches and a count of five, and so on.

Some times when we are talking to someone about Jesus and our faith, we have to go slowly. Other times, we can present information much more quickly. Sometimes our retrieval techniques require some information or a question, then a pause, before we continue, for a response or an answer.

2. If the fish aren't biting, you need to change your presentation or change the bait. Often times a bass fisherman will fish with several different colors, before he finds the one that the fish will hit. Other times it requires switching from hard baits, to plastics, or spinners, and back again before just the right one is discovered.

The same thing is true with evangelizing. Sometimes we have to switch our discussion from the Bible, to the sacraments, to the Real Presence, and back again, before we discover a person's interests.

3. The bigger the bait, the bigger the fish" isn't always true! Some of the biggest bass I have ever caught have come on smaller baits.

Sometimes subtlety works better than a two-by-four to the head. Often times, following a men's conference, the attendees will remember one line, one suggestion, or one thought, chosen from among a day's worth of material.

4. If the fish are biting on one bait, fish that bait until they quit responding. One of the joys of fishing is finding just the right bait that will work consistently all day. Fishermen are taught not to switch baits until it quits working. Sometimes, bait will quit working in a few minutes, other times the bait will work all day! I have begun many a day's fishing with a simple four-inch scoundrel natural worm, and fished it all day!

In evangelization, if an approach is working or has worked for you in the past, start there. It may work time and time again, but be careful—it might quit working just as fast.

5. **The barometer and moon phases will affect whether fish are going to bite at all.** There are just some days that the dropping barometer reading or a bad phase of the moon will prevent something good from working. You can drop the juiciest worm right in their face and they will ignore it! Fishermen are trained to understand that when this happens, it's probably a good idea to just go home.

The same is true for evangelization, some days the person you are trying to reach just isn't in the mood. Nothing that you say or do will work on him that day. As with fishermen, it is probably best to drop the subject and save your discussion for another day. It might be better to delay your discussion, rather than turn the person off, otherwise, they may never have any discussion with you about faith in the future.

Whether fishing for fish or fishing for men, the rules are the same! Isn't it great that our Lord not only understood this but chose his apostles by these traits?

Why didn't Jesus choose educated men to be his first followers? Why these fishermen?

Now you know!

Reflection: *Do you see the similarities between fishing for fish and fishing for people? Is being sensitive to the person you are evangelizing important? What do you look for when you are sharing Jesus with someone new?*

My Children Have Lost the Faith

Not a week goes by that I don't speak with someone who is distraught because their son or daughter has lost the faith, yet, it is rarely discussed in public, or preached about, and help is not offered. It is the most ignored problem, yet faced by many Christian parents. These are the faithful parents who are in the pews on Sunday. They raised their children in the faith. It is part of everything they do, yet somewhere between high school and their early 20's, they decide that religion, especially Christianity, is not for them.

They are influenced by the secular media, and college professors, who laugh at religion as something that no reasonable person would profess. They constantly attack Christianity as being outdated, old-fashioned, in conflict with science, women's rights, gay rights, and so forth.

We don't discuss it because we are embarrassed and ashamed, that maybe, somehow, we failed as parents to make our faith exciting and attractive to our adult children. I know because I have these same feelings.

What can faithful parents do? Here are a few ideas from my own experience;

1. Don't argue with them! It only pushes them farther away. You'll never out-shout or outwit your kids into believing. I can think of one particular argument that I'd love to take back!

2. Remain Faithful! Don't let their falling away from the faith discourage you or make you suppress your beliefs.

> Exodus 20:6 says, "But bestowing *mercy down to the thousandth generation*, on the

children of those who love me and keep
my commandments." — (NAB)
(Emphasis added)

Sirach 44:13 reads, "And for all time their *progeny will endure*, their glory will never be blotted out." — (NAB) (Emphasis added)

Our Lord promises that if we remain faithful, he will bless our children! But, we must remain faithful and not be afraid to show the joy of the Lord in our lives. In the book of Acts 16:3, when the jailer asked Paul and Silas, "Sirs, what must I do to be saved?" They said, "Believe in the Lord Jesus and you and *your household* will be saved." — (NAB) (Emphasis added.)

3. Prayers and Sacrifice! Saint Augustine is considered one of the greatest Christian thinkers of all time. He spent his younger days as a hedonist. He was anything but saintly! His mother, Saint Monica, prayed for decades for his return to the faith, and finally he did and became a Doctor of the Church.

4. Pray that God brings someone else (beside you) into their lives. Then trust God to do it! Although Monica prayed, she also prayed that God would intervene and put someone into Augustine's life to prompt his conversion. God did. Saint Ambrose, the bishop of Milan, was Augustine's match for rhetoric. He brought Augustine back to the faith. Monica's prayers were answered with his knowledge and wisdom.

5. Study and Learn to defend the faith! As we learn more about the faith ourselves, we are better equipped to answer questions and defend what we believe. As stated in 1 Peter 3:15, "Always be ready to give an explanation to anyone who asks you for a reason for your hope, but do it with gentleness and reverence, keeping your conscience clear, so that, when you are maligned, those who defame your good conduct in Christ may themselves be put to shame." (NAB)

6. Love them and do not push them away! Love them more than ever. Make it a point to tell them that you love them. Let them see your joy and happiness. Make them want what you have!

> This is good and pleasing to God our Savior, ***who wills everyone*** to be saved and to come to the knowledge of truth.
> — (Timothy 2:3-4, NAB) (Emphasis added)

Let's make a commitment to pray for all those who have fallen away from the faith of their youth.

Reflection: How can I communicate better with my own adult children? Do I have faith to believe what scripture says?

Healed, Not Cured

> And some men brought on a stretcher a man who was paralyzed; they were trying to bring him in and set [him] in his presence. But not finding a way to bring him in because of the crowd, they went up on the roof and lowered him on the stretcher through the tiles into the middle in front of Jesus. When he saw

their faith, he said, "As for you, your sins
are forgiven — (Luke 5:17-20, NAB)

Several years ago, a famous Baptist minister was talking with a minister in
another town. He asked if miracles and healing were part of his ministry.
The Baptist minister said that they weren't. Although he often prayed for
people, he didn't see any miracles.

Preaching a few weeks later in a church in out-of-state, he decided to offer
to pray for anyone with needs after his talk. To his surprise, several people
stayed afterwards, so patiently he met with each of them and prayed for
them.

A few days later, he received a call from a woman reminding him that he
had prayed for her husband, who had cancer that night. "Had cancer?" he
asked, hoping for a healing.

"Well, he's dead now," the woman answered!

With a sense of failure, he heard the woman continue that her husband
had come to the church that day angry at God. Angry that God let this
happen, angry that he would die soon, and his nastiness kept getting worse
and worse, that is, until the minister prayed for him. As they walked out of
church, she knew that something was different. He was calm, more
accepting, and the four days since then, were their best ever!

She then said something profound, "He wasn't cured, but he was healed!"

This story helps bring home the parable of the paralytic in Luke 5. The
men in the story had obviously heard of the miracles that Jesus was
performing and brought their friend on a stretcher to have him cured.
They even went so far as to lower him through the tiles in the roof to the
feet of Jesus, because they could not get him through the crowd.

What happened next must have surprised, astonished, and even confused the paralytic and his friends. Jesus laid hands on the man and said, "Your sins are forgiven."

What Jesus offered was forgiveness and spiritual healing. Which is more important? Being able to walk in this life or to be forgiven and be with the Lord in eternal life? They were looking for a *cure*, but instead their friend was *healed!* To prove his point, Jesus then told him to pick up his stretcher and go home!

As we live our lives, with the trials, diseases, and infirmities we experience, it's OK to pray for a cure, but more importantly, let's pray for healing! How sweet it would be to hear Jesus say, "As for you, your sins are forgiven."

Reflection: *Do you understand the difference between healing and a cure? Which is more important, that you are cured or your sins are forgiven? What do you think was going through the minds of the friends of the paralyzed man following his encounter with the Lord?*

The Sin of Partiality

My brothers, show no partiality as you adhere to the faith in our glorious Lord Jesus Christ. For if a man with gold rings on his fingers and in fine clothes comes into your assembly, and a poor person in shabby clothes also comes in, and you pay attention to the one wearing the fine

clothes and say, "Sit here, please," while
you say to the poor one, "Stand there,"
or "Sit at my feet," have you not made
distinctions among yourselves and
become judges with evil designs? Listen,
my beloved brothers. Did not God
choose those who are poor in the world
to be rich in faith and heirs of the
kingdom that he promised to those who
love him? But you dishonored the poor
person. Are not the rich oppressing you?
And do they themselves not haul you off
to court? — (James 2:1-6, NAB)

A rich celebrity walks into a restaurant with his entourage. The hostess
spots him and runs to the kitchen to tell the owner that a celebrity is in the
restaurant. Hurriedly, the owner rushes to greet the celebrity and seat him
and his group at the best table.

The chef makes an appearance at the table and offers to prepare a special
meal for the group. The waitress goes the extra mile to keep their water
and wine glasses full and the service is first class. The owner returns to the
table to inform the celebrity that dinner is on the house tonight, that he
has taken care of everything. A few hours later the entourage leaves the
restaurant, no bill and no tip for the amazing service.

That same evening, at the alley door adjacent to the kitchen, a homeless
family appears and appeals to the owner, "Can you help us? Our family has
nothing to eat. Can we have some of the left-over bread that was returned
to the kitchen uneaten or some leftover soup?"

The owner grows impatient, "We have nothing to offer you, please leave
the alley before we have to call the police!" Later, from a distance, the
hungry family watches as bread and leftover food is carted to the dumpster
as the restaurant is preparing to close for the night.

In James 2:1-4, we read the about the sin of partiality. I'll bet many have never heard of this sin. We, as Christians, are forbidden to hold the faith with partiality. But, we do. It is incompatible with our faith.

The fifth chapter of James lists five things that are wrong with showing partiality, favoritism, or prejudice;

1. In verse 1, it says that **partiality is inconsistent,** if we adhere to our faith in Jesus.
2. In verse 2, **we become judges** of who is and who isn't worthy. That's not our job as Christians.
3. In verse 5, we are asked to remember that **God favored the poor** to be rich in their faith.
4. In verse 6, we **dishonor the poor,** simply because of social or financial status.
5. In verse 9, we **violate the law** of "love thy neighbor." — (James 5:1-5, NAB)

We are all guilty of partiality. We live in a society that puts too much emphasis on celebrity, wealth, and fame, and not enough on loving thy neighbor, no matter their circumstances.

> But if you show partiality, you commit
> sin, and are convicted by the law as
> transgressors. — (James 2:9, NAB)

Let's make an effort this week to downplay celebrity and concentrate on loving our neighbor, especially those in need. Let's be conscious of our sin of partiality. It is what Jesus asks of us as his followers.

Reflection: *Have you ever been guilty of the sin of partiality? Why do we judge people in our lives as being worthy or not worthy of our love and respect?*

Chapter 3:

GOD'S GRACE AT THE HOLIDAYS

Leave It at the Altar

> Have no anxiety at all, but in everything,
> by prayer and petition, with thanksgiving,
> make your requests known to God. Then
> the peace of God that surpasses all
> understanding will guard your hearts and
> minds in Christ Jesus. — (Philippians
> 4:6-7, NAB)

Many of us are heavily burdened when we go to Mass. Even Easter, the most joyous day of the year, may be tainted by the burdens we carry.

A friend was just diagnosed with stage-four cancer, and the season seems tainted.

Another Year passes and we are still estranged from a loved one that we haven't spoken to in several years, and can't remember why.

Some experience the anger and resentment of a marriage gone badly, and the loneliness of sitting in the pew alone.

Others fear what life will be like when the Alzheimer's takes their spouse.

Sometimes it seems that these burdens are just too big to handle.

Psalm 55 tells you to, "cast your care upon the LORD, who will give you support. He will never allow the righteous to stumble." (NAB)

Today is the best day of the year to cast your fears, burdens, pain, anger, resentment, to the Lord. It's time to "let go, and Let God."

It's time to leave it at the altar! It is time to release these feelings to a God who will never allow us to stumble. It's time to unburden ourselves of these problems that eat away at us.

Today, as you approach the altar to receive Communion, what problem are you going to leave at the altar? Why not pray a prayer of release, asking God to take these burdens from you and bring you peace.

> Lord, I release every problem to you,
> burdens that I can't handle myself. I lay
> my fears, pain, anger, resentment at the
> foot of the cross. My fear of losing a
> loved one…I leave at the altar.
> The anger I feel from being wrongfully
> accused….I leave at the altar.
> The resentment of being passed over for
> a promotion at work….I leave at the
> altar.
> The pain of getting out of bed....I leave
> at the altar.

Today, at Mass, let go and let God. Let's lay our burdens at the foot of the cross.

Take my heart, loving Father, as I put it on your altar. I put all my burdens in your loving care.

Do this, and watch what happens!

Reflections: *What burdens are you laying at the altar this Sunday? Do you place your burdens in God's loving care? How can we use these thoughts to have a happier life?*

A Giving Heart

> When he looked up he saw some wealthy people putting their offerings into the treasury and he noticed a poor widow putting in two small coins. He said, "I tell you truly, this poor widow put in more than all the rest; for those others have all made offerings from their surplus wealth, but she, from her poverty, has offered her whole livelihood. — (Luke 21:1-4, NAB)

There is a story of a young girl who was moved by the request of her preacher a few weeks before Christmas. The preacher mentioned from the pulpit there was a family in their very small congregation that was down on their luck. The father was unemployed, the oldest child was ill, and every penny they had could hardly keep the family together.

"Wouldn't it be nice," he offered, "if the congregation would all bring in what they could next Sunday and present it to this wonderful family."

The young girl was determined to do whatever she could that week and would bring in any money she could accumulate to help them.

She tapped her piggy bank; she looked for loose change in the sofa cushions, and helped a neighbor with some chores to earn another dollar. All in all, she accumulated $2.73.

The next Sunday, as she walked down the center isle to drop off her $2.73 in the basket, she felt humble; embarrassed that she could only give this needy family less than 3 dollars.

At the end of the service, the preacher called the family up to the front to present the money that congregation had collected. To the young girls' amazement, it was her family!

By the time I heard this story from that young girl fifty years had passed and she was a successful business woman. She told the story from a banquet podium the night she was honored for her philanthropy.

Her story reminded me of the poor widow's two small coins. She was generous even though she had very little to give.

As Jesus explained, generosity has nothing to do with a person's financial situation. A generous person is generous whether they are rich or poor.

In my experience, some of the most generous people I ever met were people with very limited means. They give out of the kindness of their hearts, they give to be a blessing, they give out of a sense of gratitude, and they work so that they can have a chance to give. They realize that it is impossible to love without giving.

They truly have the heart of a giver. They realize that giving increases their happiness. They don't give in order to get. They have no selfish motives. In fact, they often give anonymously so as not to draw attention to themselves.

If I asked for a list of the most Christ-like persons you know, many would say my grandma, my mom, a special aunt, my father, or grandfather. The reason? They have a generous heart.

What can we do to have a giving heart? We can start by counting our blessings. Gratitude leads to generosity when we realize that no matter our circumstances, someone is suffering more.

Let's make it a goal to have a giving heart!

Reflections: Who are the most Christ-like people you know? Do you believe that generosity has little to do with the amount of money involved? How do we measure our generosity?

Even Now

> Yet *even now*—oracle of the LORD—
> return to me with your **whole
> heart,** with fasting, weeping, and
> mourning. Rend your hearts, not your
> garments, and return to the LORD, your
> God, For he is gracious and merciful,
> slow to anger, abounding in steadfast
> love, and relenting in punishment." —
> (Joel 2:12-13, NAB), (emphasis added.)

There is something very appealing about Lent. It calls us to cleanse something from within, to burn away those things that keep us from a wholehearted relationship with God.

That is why there are often more people at Mass on Ash Wednesday than on any given Sunday. Those ashes are a symbol, an outward sign of this cleansing.

The real work of Lent is not about shaming ourselves; it's not about a guilt trip for our sins. Lent offers us a sense of reconnection, of returning to God wholeheartedly; it's about moving forward, leaving our past sins behind and having a deeper relationship with Jesus Christ.

> For he says: "In an acceptable time I
> heard you, and on the day of salvation I
> helped you. Behold, now is a very
> acceptable time; behold, now is the day
> of salvation." — (2 Corinthians 6:2,
> NAB)

Now is an acceptable time to get started. Even now, we can stop resisting a relationship with God, and follow him. Not in a superficial way, but with our whole heart.

Even now…..what seems hopeless in your life can be made whole.
Even now…..your marriage on the brink of divorce can be restored.
Even now…..your children who have left the faith can return.
Even now…..your job search can end with a new beginning.
Even now…..your cancer can go into remission.
Even now…..if only we return to the Lord with our WHOLE heart.

Be encouraged. In Matthew 7:8 we are told, "For everyone who asks, receives; and the one who seeks, finds; and to the one who knocks, the door will be opened." (NAB) It's guaranteed!

Want to get closer to Our Lord? Then, we need to spend some time with Him. Let's really try to put into place the tenants of Lent; prayer, fasting and almsgiving. Let's take some time during Lent to make it a point to love God more wholeheartedly. Here are a few things you can do.

Attend Mass. Not only every Sunday, but during Lent why not try to add another Mass during the week. There are many churches that offer Mass early morning, or in the evening. I like to attend Mass during my lunch hour. Try to attend at least one service during Holy Week.

Increase your prayer time. There are always moments you can find to pray. I like praying in the car on my way to and from work. It helps me be in a better place when I get to work, and prayer relieves the stress of the day on my way home.

Read scripture, a good book, or a Lenten devotional. There are some really good Lenten books and devotionals that can help you in your attempt to be more wholehearted in your relationship with God.

Give up something that will help another. It is one thing to give up that double latte, but then donate the money saved over the 40 days to your favorite charity.

Get involved in a service project. The local St. Vincent DePaul Society, Salvation Army, a homeless shelter, or a warming station could always use an extra hand.

Let's make this the best Lent ever. Let's take the time to love Our Lord wholeheartedly, so that at Easter when we proclaim, "He is Risen," we can all declare with love and conviction, "Alleluia!"

Reflections: *What can you do even now to make Lent more meaningful? What do you think of this list of things to do? Are you trying to make this the best Lent ever?*

I gave it up for Lent

> Fasting makes sense if it really chips away at our security and, as a consequence, benefits someone else, if it helps us cultivate the style of the Good Samaritan, who bent down to his brother in need and took care of him. - (Pope Francis, 2015)

Every year, I spend a good part of the month of March in Naples, Florida, with my wife, Diane. Naples is a wonderful place, very upscale, with lots of retirees who have had successful careers.

Last year, at Ash Wednesday Mass, the priest mentioned during the homily that he had received several calls in the previous few days asking him about the rules for fasting.

"How old do you have to be excused from fasting?" was the question.

"Well," said the priest, "it is 59 years of age which includes 99 percent of you!"

He went on to give a great homily on what fasting should be about. At the end of Mass before the concluding hymn, he reminded all in attendance that we abstain from meat on Ash Wednesday. He said, "If you are at the Turtle Club tonight for dinner, don't order the sixteen ounce steak!"

That night, we just happened to have reservations at that very restaurant and as we sat waiting for our waiter to finish taking an order at a nearby table, we couldn't help but overhear the conversation.

"I'll have the New York Strip," said the elderly gentleman.

"No, honey!" his wife exclaimed. "Father said not to have the steak tonight."

"OK then," he replied, as he looked at the waiter, "I'll have the lobster instead!"

Apparently, the priest's message lost something of its meaning in the hours that followed Mass.

It reminded me of myself as a kid. I'd give up candy for Lent, only to gorge myself on chocolate Easter bunnies, Peeps and marshmallow Easter eggs from my overstuffed basket on Easter morning.

Another time I gave up broccoli and asparagus, both of which I dislike, and watermelon, which is out of season during Lent!

It's hard to admit, but I seemed to have missed a similar homily years ago.

That is the problem I have with rule-book Catholicism. We are so fixated on following the rules that we miss the reason for the tradition. It has nothing to do with our age or finding the right loophole; it's about trying to have our best Lent ever!

It's about taking the three pillars of Lent, prayer, fasting and almsgiving, and making them more meaningful in your life.

It's about giving up your smart phone in the evening to spend more quality time with your family.

It's about giving up Facebook and using that time to read an uplifting book, commit to a daily devotional, saying a rosary, or praying the Stations of the Cross.

It's about giving up complaining, gossiping, or meaningless texting. Instead, volunteer at the food pantry.

It's about giving up that double mocha latte and donating the money saved to a charity.

Most people give up the same thing every year, and truth be told, if you fit into that category, then you need to do something different if you are going to have a meaningful Lenten season.

Try doing something you haven't done before, something different, something out of character for you. It will have so much more meaning.

Giving up chocolate, soda pop, alcohol, or fast foods may meet the minimum requirements; but we should ask the question that Pope Francis suggested in his 2014 Ash Wednesday homily, "Does my fasting benefit someone else?"

Then, our Lenten fast won't be all about us, but about being like the Good Samaritan.

This year let's take some time and think about what we really want to get from Lent this year. Let's think about how our spiritual life can grow as we prepare to have our best Easter ever.

Reflections: What are you giving up for Lent? What can you do differently this year to have your best Lent ever? How about doing something different this year

Love Covers a Multitude of Sins

Above all, let your love for one another
be intense, because love covers a
multitude of sins. — (1 Peter 4:8, NAB)

Hatred stirs up disputes, but love covers
all offenses. — (Proverbs 10:12, NAB)

The call of Lent is to turn away from sin, to commit to prayer and devotion that will bring us closer to God as we prepare for the death and resurrection of our Lord and Savior Jesus Christ.

It also calls us to a greater human kindness and a sense of charity to others. It begs us to realize that our sins are no less sinful that those of others around us.

In 1 Peter, we are asked to have such an intense love for one another that our love will cover a multitude of sins. What is meant by "covering" sin?

First, it doesn't mean we ignore sin, not at all. However, if we have an attitude of forgiveness, we must ask ourselves if this is an offense we should let go of.

When someone offends us or sins against us, we have two choices, to overlook the offense or to address it. It doesn't make the offense any less a sin, but the Bible is asking us to overlook some sins against us, to "cover them."

It's not that we condone the sin or pretend that it doesn't exist, but that in spite of failures and faults we choose to love the offender, to refrain from judging them on this one offense and not let this indiscretion ruin our relationship.

We can "cover" others by always assuming the best of everyone. That means not gossiping, or sharing their sins with others. Love covers bad decisions, selfish, stupid, shameful, unwise decisions. It doesn't lessen the sin, but in Christian charity it gives the offender the benefit of the doubt and offers a second chance.

When Jesus confronted the adulterous woman, he didn't condemn her as the scribes and Pharisees did, demanding that she be stoned to death.

On the contrary, he asked those without sin to cast the first stone. And, when no one stepped up to cast a stone, Jesus "covered" her sin with love.

He acknowledged her sin and told her to go and sin no more. His was an attitude of forgiveness, the attitude we should have too.

She replied, "No one, sir." Then Jesus said, "Neither do I condemn you. Go, [and] from now on do not sin anymore." — (John 8:11, NAB)

This Lent, let's make an effort to be less judgmental, to be aware of our own sinfulness and not be so quick to point out the sins of others.

How can we accomplish this?

First, we need to not sweat the small stuff. We should always take a moment and ask ourselves if this is an offense that I should just let go of and cover with love?

This doesn't mean we ignore the sin but if we must address it do it privately and don't discuss their sins with others.

Secondly, we should assume the best in others. Let's try to give our family members, friends, fellow workers, and people we meet the benefit of the doubt and be more charitable in our judgment.

Finally, after serious thought and reflection decide to overlook it or address it. If we do feel it necessary to address it, let's take a lead from Jesus and do it quietly, discreetly, and with great love.

Lent, is a time to reflect on our own sinfulness, our own shortcomings, our own selfish, shameful, and unwise decisions. In doing so, we will become more charitable, less judgmental, and forgiving. Isn't that what Lent is all about?

We can do it, my friend. That's my prayer today.

Reflections: *How are we called to a greater human kindness? What do we mean by covering sin? What is an attitude of forgiveness?*

On Father's Day

Father's Day, it is the one day each year that we honor fathers, a day to tell Dad just how much he means to us. It is a shame that over 24 million kids, one in three, growing up in the United States today, have no father present in the household to honor. At the current rate, over 50 percent will be growing up in a fatherless household in a few generations. Nine out of ten American parents see this as a crisis. There is a "father factor" in nearly all of the social issues facing America today.

Where is the outrage? What are we doing about it? Why are men abandoning their responsibilities?

Fatherhood is in crisis in America. The statistics are alarming. Children growing up in fatherless homes are:

- More likely to be poor.
- More likely to be incarcerated.
- More likely to abuse drugs and alcohol.
- More likely to have a teen pregnancy.
- More likely to have problems in school.

Is that what we want for our kids?

To have a father might just be the biggest factor in dealing with the greatest social issues facing American today.

So, where are these fathers? How do we reach them? How do we tell them that anyone can have a child, but it takes a man to be a father?

Some may be so self-absorbed that they just can't handle a family. Others might have endured physical or psychological abuse as children and fear they will be abusive as well. Still others may have come from fatherless homes themselves and have no role model for fatherhood or doubt their ability to parent.

As Christian fathers, we need to look for opportunities to mentor these young men.

Our local pregnancy center began a men's ministry to reach out not only to young pregnant women, but the father as well. That's a start.

Our jail ministry group often talks to incarcerated men about "manning up" and understanding the responsibility of fatherhood.

Our schools need to realize that teaching parenting may be more important than just about any other subject.

Community centers and recreational facilities need to use sports to begin a dialogue on fatherhood.

We need to find these men where they are and bring the message to them that fatherhood might just be the most important thing they do in their lifetime.

Today, let's truly honor those who are doing their best to be good fathers. They work hard every day to be present for their children and spouse. They take this responsibility seriously. Here are a few things to consider.

1. **Great fatherhood begins with a relationship with a child's mother.** The way Dad treats Mom becomes the blueprint for how our sons will treat their wives and will provide a role model for our daughters as to what to look for in a husband of their own.
2. **We need to spend time with our kids.** Kids spell the word father, T-I-M-E! Time just being together, playing, discovering, and bonding.
3. **We need to nurture and guide.** We need to provide a moral compass based on our faith. It will serve them and future generations to come.
4. **We need to protect and provide** for their health and well-being. Kids need to feel safe and secure knowing that dad will protect them.
5. **We are their first and most important role model.** Remember, they are watching.

> Heavenly Father,
> Help me to become a better father.
> Make the way I treat their mother be a
> model for their future relationships.
> May I find quality time to spend with my
> children and understand that "any time"

is better than waiting for the "right time."
May I nurture and guide my children, passing along my faith by making God, church, and service to others, a priority. Lord, give me the ability to provide for my wife and children and protect them from any harm.
And, may my kids look at me as a shining example of God's love, that one day they will say, "I want to be just like Dad!
Amen.

Happy Father's Day!

Reflections: *Fathers, how do your kids view your relationship with their mother? What do you think of the idea that kids spell father T-I-M-E? Do you view yourself as a role model?*

Welcome to Secular Advent

And do this because you know the time; it is the hour now for you to awake from sleep. For our salvation is nearer now than when we first believed; the night is advanced, the day is at hand. Let us then throw off the works of darkness [and]

put on the armor of light. — (Romans
13:11-12, NAB)

Welcome my friends to Secular Advent! For those of you who are not familiar with the holiday season, it began several years ago and has grown into the biggest secular holiday of the year.

Secular Advent used to begin on Black Friday. Now it begins with Grey Thursday, right after Thanksgiving dinner, Greed can't wait for an entire day of giving thanks, especially when we forget who to thank!

There are other minor holidays during Secular Advent. Holidays like Small Business Saturday and Cyber Monday. Secular Advent continues all the way until Return Unwanted Gifts Week!

For those of you who celebrate the Christian Advent know that Secular Advent is the antithesis of this.

Secular Advent asks us to speed up and spend money now! Christian Advent asks us to slow down and prepare for the coming of our savior Jesus Christ.

Secular Advent asks us to spend money we don't have on things we don't need, under the pretense that "it was on sale!" Christian Advent asks us to be thankful for what we have and to give to those who have little.

Secular Advent asks us to fight for our rights for the last big screen television at Walmart. We must fight even if it means we have to kill for it, or at least start a riot. Christian Advent asks us to pray for peace in the world.

Secular Advent reminds us that seven year-old's need an iPhone, an Xbox and Play Station gaming systems. After all, they deserve it. Christian

Advent reminds us that some children will have no gifts at Christmas. Wouldn't it be nice to buy something for a child who has little or nothing?

As for me, I prefer the Advent of our Christian faith. And, so as not to get caught up in the hype of this secular holiday, here are a few things I am going to do. Maybe you might try these too:

I'm going to *slow down and enjoy the advent season*. I'll enjoy the beauty of winter closing in, snowfall, and family and friends.

As a Catholic, I'm going to *attend mass every day* during advent season. I'll focus on the coming of Jesus, not only on Christmas day, but his second coming as well.

I'm going *to increase my prayer time*. I'll especially to pray for those who will be sad because they have lost a loved one this year.

I'm going to *help someone in need*, a family member, a friend or just a name from the giving tree or Salvation Army list.

My protest will be a quiet one, a silent one. I will just choose not to take part in the madness. Instead, I'll try to concentrate my thoughts and deeds on throwing off the works of darkness and putting on the armor of light.

Please join me this Advent.

Reflections: What has happened to the real meaning of the Advent season? Have you found yourself getting swept away in the commercialism? What can we do to keep the real meaning of the season alive?

The Empty Chair

He will wipe every tear from their eyes,
and there shall be no more death or
mourning, wailing or pain, [for] the old
order has passed away. — (Revelations
21:4, NAB)

The LORD is close to the
brokenhearted, saves those whose spirit
is crushed. — (Psalm 34:1, NAB)

Thanksgiving and Christmas are the happiest times of the year. We get
together with family and friends, exchange gifts, share wonderful meals,
and enjoy the holidays.

But, for many of us, the loss of a loved one makes this a sad and even
depressing time. Let's face it; every one of us will have a holiday where
there is an empty chair.

The loss of a spouse, parent, grandparent, or a child can be devastating
enough, but the holidays have a way of magnifying the sadness. Add the
cold and snow and the fact that it gets dark earlier, and just getting out of
the house seems like an insurmountable task.

So, what can we do? How can we not only get through the holidays, but
find joy in the season?

Here are some ideas that might help:

1. **Let the traditions evolve.** If you have always hosted Christmas at your house, let someone else host. Especially for those who have lost a spouse, this is the perfect time to pass on the hosting responsibilities to an adult daughter or son. After all, they have families, and starting a new Christmas tradition will take the pressure off of you and let you think less of what was and more of right now and what can be.

2. **During the Holiday season manage your loneliness.** Stay active and get out of the house. Accept invitations from friends, even if you don't feel quite up to it. Try volunteering at a homeless shelter, or help serve Thanksgiving dinner to the less fortunate in your town.

3. **Accept your feelings, it's OK to grieve.** A wonderful way to remember a lost loved one is to light a candle, hang their favorite Christmas ornament on the tree, or make a charitable donation in their name. Feel free to talk about your loved one with family at the holidays. They too want to keep the deceased's spirit alive and part of family traditions. It gives them permission to share some wonderful stories or photos that will warm your heart.

4. **Take care of your health.** During these difficult times it is easy to slack off in your self-care. Get up, shower, get dressed, work out, take a walk, and attend Mass or anything else to get moving. Remember to eat regular meals. Often, the loneliness of the holidays causes us to miss meals, eat all of the wrong things, or to drink too much coffee or alcohol.

5. **Stay close to Our Lord.** As Psalm 34 reminds us, the Lord is close to the brokenhearted. He is there for us at Mass, in the reception of the sacraments, in the rosary, and in the reading scriptures. He will get us through these difficult times if we just reach out in prayer.

That is the message of Christmas. We are not alone, not when the night is darkest, the wind coldest, or the world seemingly most indifferent.

With God's help, we can make it through the holidays together, and celebrate our lost loved one whose memory remains, in spite of the empty chair.

God bless you my friend.

Reflections: *What do you think of Tony's ideas for remembering a loved one? Do you have a tradition at the holidays to remember those that have past? What can we do to help a person who has experienced a loss this year?*

✥

Our Thanksgiving Pizza

A man gave a great dinner to which he invited many. When the time for the dinner came, he dispatched his servant to say to those invited, "Come, everything is now ready." But one by one, they all began to excuse themselves. — (Luke 14:16-18, NAB)

In June, Diane and I celebrated our 46th wedding anniversary. In those 46 years, we have had some interesting holiday gatherings but none like the one in Atlanta, Georgia, that never happened.

We were a young married couple and seeking a new adventure in Atlanta. I had just received a job offer to program one of the first talk radio stations in the country, Ring Radio.

I can still remember our drive to Atlanta. We followed each other down I-85, she in her Monte Carlo and me in my Honda Civic. We were young and very inexperienced. Diane had barely been out of the state of Ohio and our honeymoon was the first time either of us had been out of the country.

In Atlanta, we made friends quickly. Many folks were just like us, northerners who had come to the south for work. All had left families in places like Ohio, Michigan, Pennsylvania, and Wisconsin and had to make friends in our new environment or be alone. So, people were very friendly.

Diane and I joined the local Catholic Church, a small gathering of mostly northerners that met for Mass in a small activity center with an Irish priest, a missionary to the US! It was 1975 and Vietnam was still fresh in the countries consciousness. I was in the Army Reserves and had drill weekends in Rome, Georgia, as well as summer camps in Wisconsin, and Virginia. One of our church's outreaches was to adopt a few South Vietnamese families, who had settled in our area.

Life in Atlanta was going pretty well until we realized that we would not be going home for Thanksgiving. My new job meant that we would be celebrating the holiday away from our family in Ohio. Then, Diane had a great idea!

"I am sure that there are other couples like us who won't be making it home to their families this Thanksgiving, so let's host a big Thanksgiving dinner here."

"That's a great idea," I exclaimed! I could already taste Diane's great cooking.

We invited four other couples to join us, and everyone accepted. Diane prepared the menu, we bought a turkey, and I received a holiday ham from my employer; there would be plenty of food for everyone.

The day before our big feast, one of the couples called to tell us they wouldn't be making it to the dinner. Her husband was able to get last-minute plane tickets and they were going home to Michigan. Well, there were still three couples joining us.

That night, while Diane was making preparations and doing some baking, the phone rang, and you guessed it, another couple called to cancel. "Boy, there sure is going to be a lot of food for six people," I said with a little disappointment in my voice.

Thanksgiving morning, the phone rang twice more, each with the same news that our guests would be spending Thanksgiving somewhere else. We were in shock! The expectations of the good food shared with friends vanished as I hung up the phone for the final time.

The next hour or so was spent with shared tears and disappointment. Now what? What do we do with a turkey, a ham, and all the side dishes and desserts?

Then, Diane had another idea.

"Let's box it all up and deliver it to the Vietnamese families our church has sponsored. They can celebrate our U.S. holiday with their families," she said choking back tears. "At least someone will be having a family holiday." We did just that.

It is difficult to describe the amazed look on the faces of the Vietnamese families as we dropped off our American feast. Although they were still learning English, their tearful thank you, head bows, and smiles were all we needed to know that we were not only doing the right thing, but that somehow God was directing the entire story.

When we returned to our apartment, we realized that it was late and we still had not eaten. "What do you want on the pizza?" I asked, as I dialed the local pizza shop. "Pepperoni and green peppers," she replied. Thirty minutes later we were enjoying our Thanksgiving meal, alone, but laughing, glad to be together, and somehow knowing that God had used us to deliver a miracle to families who will forever remember their first Thanksgiving Day.

Reflections: *Have you ever felt that God was directing your actions? Do you remember a time when things didn't go as planned? How did you react?*

Your Presence is Your Present

> And the Word became flesh and made his dwelling among us, and we saw his glory, the glory as of the Father's only Son, full of grace and truth. — (John 1:14)

At our Christmas Mass at the jail Tuesday night, the celebrant Father Lee, a humble, on-fire dynamo from South Korea, said something in the homily that resonated with me. He said, "Your presence is your present."

As kids, presents are an important part of the Christmas season. Looking through toy catalogs, watching television for the newest must-have toys, and dreaming of Santa Claus placing them under the tree, is at the center of the season.

As we get older, the present isn't quite as important as the people we have around us. Family and friends become very important at Christmas time. There is not a parent alive that wouldn't trade even the biggest present for having their family together at the holidays. Sons and daughters, grand-kids, and friends, are the best Christmas gifts. Their presence at your holiday is the best Christmas present you could receive.

Our being present, is the greatest gift we can give, as well. I mean being "really present" and attentive to what is happening to them in their lives, and not allowing our attention to drift to our job, health, or any other distraction. Being truly present!

It is said that there are three elements to giving; the giver, the recipient, and the gift itself. The least important is the gift. The interaction of the two people involved, their presence to each other is the real gift.

We have seen recently how a lifetime of gifts can disappear instantly, like the homes and belongings of the people affected by Hurricane Sandy, or worse yet, the loss of the "presence" of the 20 children and 6 teachers at Sandy Hook Elementary School in Connecticut. Their presence is only a memory now.

At Christmas, it is good to remember that God gave us a gift too, the gift of His presence in the gift of His Son, Jesus Christ. He became man, dwelt among us, sharing His presence with his family, His friends, the Apostles, and the people he touched during His ministry.

Jesus is still present today. Let us strive to be attentive to our Lord this Christmas as well, and make it a point to spend more time with Him, in praise, prayer, and adoration. Pray with me:

> Lord, make me more attentive to the
> presence of the people around me this
> Christmas, my wife, children, and
> friends. Let me not be distracted by the
> hurried pace of the things of the secular
> world that are not important. Help me,
> Lord, to be more attentive to you as well,
> in my prayer life and in helping those less
> fortunate around me. Help me to spend
> this Christmas, attentive to the presence
> of the Holy Family, and my own family,
> this day. Their presence will be the best
> present I receive this Christmas.

God bless you. May you have a blessed and merry Christmas, and a happy and healthy New Year!

Reflection: *Do you agree that receiving a present at Christmas isn't as important as the people around us? What can we do to shut out the secular pressure to buy more presents? Which is most important, the gift, the giver, or the recipient? How do you relate to Jesus as God's gift to use at Christmas? What can you do to keep Christ in Christmas?*

My Christmas Train

> Amen, I say to you, unless you turn and become like children, you will not enter the kingdom of heaven. Whoever humbles himself like this child is the greatest in the kingdom of heaven. And whoever receives one child such as this in my name receives me. — (Matthew 18:3-5, NAB)

One of my oldest childhood Christmas memories (reinforced by an annual recall by my parents) was when I was six years old. All I wanted for Christmas was a Lionel Train set that I had been admiring in the 1954 Lionel catalog. On Christmas morning, there it was, along with other toys and the obligatory socks and underwear.

Before I opened the box, my parents sat me down and told me that a neighbor boy's father had been laid off and his Mom and Dad couldn't afford presents for my friend. Wouldn't it be nice if I gave up one of my toys, so that he would have something under his Christmas tree?

Quite a load to drop on a six-year-old! I thought it was a good idea and I figured I could go a while longer with the socks and underwear I owned.

"What should I do?" I asked. My Dad responded, "Think about what gift would make him the happiest and give him that one."

After a long pause, a few choked back tears, I decided that it was the train set that would make him happy and reluctantly I said, "It was the one thing I really wanted for Christmas, but it would be the gift that would make him happy, so he can have my train."

The proud look on my parents face is something I remember to this day.

As my Dad removed the train set box from under the tree, I began to open my gifts. As I torn the paper from the underwear, I noticed behind the tree a Lionel box, just like the one I had given up. It was the train set from the 1954 catalog that I wanted so badly!

My Dad had a good year at work, and was able to purchase two train sets, one for me and one for my friend. Giving up the toy was just a test to see if I would be willing to give mine up for someone in need. I realized that I had passed their unusual test and was relieved that I didn't offer up the socks instead.

Before you nominate me for sainthood, I have learned over the years that most six-year-olds would pass this test. I constantly hear stories of proud parents telling of the compassion and selflessness of their young children.

So why only a few years later, do the same children complain, "It's not fair, *everyone* has a cell phone! I want one too!" Or, "I'm the only kid I know that doesn't have an X-Box 360!"

It's the greedy, self-centered, modern world. We are barraged with Hollywood images of over indulgences. I wondered, is this new or has this been going on for a long time?

As I thought about it, I was reminded of the nativity story. In all of Bethlehem, not a single man or woman was willing to give up their bed for a pregnant woman who was about to give birth. Not one! It says something about how we see a need and ignore it.

I wonder what would happen if you posed this question to a six-year-old at Christmas, "If you knew that Mary had nowhere to go to have her baby, would you be willing to give them your bed for a night so Jesus could be born in comfort?"

I bet they would all pass the test!

Over the years, I have kept that train set, still in the original box. It has moved with me from apartment to apartment, and home to home, always reminding me that we must become like children and humble ourselves, if we truly believe in the message of the incarnation. What are you willing to give up?

Reflection: *Do you think that the six-year-old in your life would pass the test? How about your teenagers? Have you ever given up something that you wanted to help another in need? How did that make you feel?*

A Christmas Story: A $20 Shine

If a man is called to be a street sweeper, he should sweep streets even as Michelangelo painted, or Beethoven composed music, or Shakespeare wrote poetry. He should sweep streets so well that all the hosts of heaven and earth will pause to say, 'Here lived a great street sweeper who did his job well.' — (Martin Luther King Jr., 2013)

After weeks of shopping, hanging ornaments, planning meals, and making arrangements for flights home, Christmas is finally here. The pressure, anxiety, and worry will soon be over. It's so easy to get caught up in the hoopla and anticipation that we overlook the most important elements of the holiday.

As I was searching for something to write about this Christmas, something that might make this a better Christmas for you and me, I have to admit I was so stressed that nothing came to mind. These were the thoughts that went through my mind as I made the first of three trips to the airport on Christmas Eve.

I arrived about 15 minutes before my son Matthew's flight was to arrive from Orlando. As I walked through the terminal, I passed an older gentleman in a stocking cap.

As our eyes met, we exchanged Merry Christmas greetings, and as we passed each other, he looked down and said in a confident voice, "I can put a Christmas shine on those shoes for you."

Surprised, I replied, "Maybe later, I've got to check on my son's flight."

As I sat down outside the restricted area waiting for his arrival, I looked up and there was a shoe shine stand a few yards away, and standing next to the stand was the gentleman with whom I had just exchanged Christmas greetings.

As he spotted me he smiled and asked, "Ready for that Christmas shine now?"

"Sure," I replied with a smile. "I've got about 15 minutes before my son's flight arrives.

As I climbed up to the seat on his stand, it felt great as I realized that this was the first time I'd had a chance to sit all day.

"How are you," I offered making small talk.

"Blessed, I'm very blessed," he replied.

With that he began to tell me that he was just released from the hospital a week ago and this was his first day back on the job. He had heart problems and wasn't expected to make it.

"It's a miracle that I am alive today and I am so grateful," he humbly said. "Now, it's Christmas Eve and I'm alive, my wife is home cooking, and my children and grandchildren will be at my house on Christmas day. This week could have been very sad, but God has blessed me with a second chance at life, and this will be the best Christmas ever!"

As he applied the polish and brushed away at my shoes, they began to take on a shine.

"Wow!" I exclaimed. "They look shinier than when I bought them."

"I'm just getting started," He replied. "Most shoe shine stands just brush and buff; I'll give them a spit shine."

As he continued to apply coats of polish and snap his cloth, I asked, "How long have you been shining shoes?"

"Fifty-three years," he responded without missing a beat of the rhythm of the snapping cloth. "I started when I was 9 years old and I'm sixty-two now. I am proud of the job I do; I think I am the best in the business!"

After a few finishing touches, he was done, and I agreed that this was the best shoe shine I had ever seen. As I stepped down from the stand our eyes met again.

He questioned me, "Does that look like a $5 dollar shine to you?"

"No," I said. "It looks more like a $20 dollar shine to me." I reached for my wallet and handed him a $20 dollar bill.

"Merry Christmas," he said humbly.

"A blessed Christmas to you, your wife, and family too!" I quietly responded as I noticed that my son's flight had just arrived.

Later that evening, as I stood near the manger in our living room, I began to reflect on our conversation.

I, too, have had health scares and was here to enjoy the holiday.

I, too, am grateful to be alive.

My wife was cooking, baking, and preparing for Christmas Day.

I've been at a job I love for fifty years this coming January, and just like the shoe shine man, I feel that I am the best at what I do.

Standing before the manger scene, I realized that his humble gratitude had rubbed off on me, just as the dust and grime had been rubbed off my shoes. He had shined my heart at the same time he shined my shoes.

As my head bowed, a tear fell from my face onto my newly shined shoes, and I could feel God's love shining in my heart.

That's my Christmas wish for you, my friend. May you be grateful to be alive, to be spending time with your family, and proud of the work you do to support them, whether you are a doctor or a shoe shine man.

May the light of our Savior, Jesus Christ, the light of the world, shine in your heart, like the glow in my heart and the gleam of my $20 dollar shine.

Reflections: Have you ever had an experience that made you appreciate what you have? What can we learn from the shoe shine man? What is it about Christmas that makes us more appreciative?

Forgiveness, the Greatest Gift

> If you forgive others their transgressions,
> your heavenly Father will forgive you.
> But if you do not forgive others, neither
> will your Father forgive your
> transgressions. —Matthew 6:14-15,
> NAB)

In just a few days, we will celebrate Christmas. In anticipation of the holiday, we look forward to being united with family and friends. We hustle to purchase and wrap the final presents. We prepare for the great meal we will share. We can't wait to continue the family traditions that have become an integral part of the season.

We recheck our shopping list and stress out over the possibility that we might have forgotten someone, someone that we love.

Could we be forgetting someone that we once loved, someone that hurt us, someone that we may have hurt? Is there someone that you haven't forgiven or asked to forgive you?

Yes, we try to put the incident or situation out of our mind, but somehow, at Christmas, it all comes back to us. And, it limits the joy and happiness that Jesus' birth should bring us. We are locked in a prison of unforgiveness.

In a spiritual sense, the greatest gift we have ever received from God, our Heavenly Father, is His Son, Jesus Christ. He became man, destined to suffer, die on the cross, and rise again for the forgiveness of our sins. Through Jesus, we are forgiven!

> In this is love: not that we have loved
> God, but that he loved us and sent his
> Son as expiation for our sins. Beloved, if
> God so loved us, we also must love one
> another. — (John 1 4:9-10)

That forgiveness comes with a price—we must forgive too! As Jesus's death on the cross unlocks the chains of our sinfulness, we are empowered by the Holy Spirit to forgive those who have hurt us.

So, who is it? Who is the one person in most need of your forgiveness? Whether you visit them, call them, e-mail them, or send a text message, forgive them! Isn't it time to put the past behind you? Isn't it time to look ahead, with our eye on the prize of heaven and everlasting life. Isn't it time for forgiveness?

Unlock the prison of unforgiveness that burdens your heart this time of year. Then, the celebration of Christ's birth will bring you joy and happiness greater than you ever imagined. It might just be the one gift you'll remember for a lifetime.

Merry Christmas!

Reflections: *Is there someone missing from your holiday because of a fight or misunderstanding years ago? Do you have a family member that has been hurtful that needs your forgiveness this Christmas? Do you see the point about forgiveness being a gift?*

Behold!

> The next day he saw Jesus coming
> toward him and said, '**Behold**, the Lamb
> of God, who takes away the sin of the
> world.' — (John 1:29, NAB, emphasis
> added)

> The angel said to them, 'Do not be
> afraid; for behold, I proclaim to you
> good news of great joy that will be for all
> the people." — (Luke 2:10, NAB)

> And behold, I am with you always, until
> the end of the age. – (Matthew 28:20,
> NAB)

One of my favorite words from the bible is *behold.* In some older translations it is use almost 1300 times. Many of the newer translations use the word less. The meaning is never more relevant than in this distracted world we live in today.

Everyone is distracted. Soccer practice, school plays, and gymnastics; it is a wonder we can behold anything.

Many people are disgusted with social media. They are contemplating taking a break from Facebook, Instagram, Twitter, and others platforms. Advent is the perfect time to do this. When you consider that the average person spends close to three hours a day with social media, "I just don't have the time" seems like a poor excuse.

Advent is just a month away and a great time for each of us to spend some time to reflect on our relationship with our Lord. We need to find some time to behold!

To behold means to give something our undivided attention. Take our relationship with God.

Luke asks us to ponder the angel's statement to Mary to *behold* the good news.

In John's gospel, John the Baptist asks us to *behold* the Lamb of God, Who takes away the sins of the world.

And, Jesus' statement in Matthew to *behold* the fact that He will be with us always until the end of time.

Many people think that Lent is the time of year for reflection, but Advent is equally a time for reflection, a time to prepare ourselves for the coming of our Lord on Christmas day. Let's promise ourselves that we will spend some time pondering the Word of God. Let's reflect on our relationship with the Lord. And, take a needed break from social media and the distractions in our daily lives.

So, how do we do it? How do we make some time for God?

1. We need to cut back on social media! Try going on Facebook only twice a day, and shut off the notifications from Facebook and other social media platforms. If you are like most people, you can gain an hour throughout the day to just behold!
2. Use you time in the car driving to and home from work as a time of prayer and reflection. It will make your workday less stressful, and you will return home in a good mood.

3. Read at least one good inspirational book during advent. There are many wonderful Catholic and Christian authors. A visit to your favorite book store should help you find something that suits your needs.
4. Spend some quiet time in prayer and reflection each day. Try to make a weekly Holy Hour, or attend a weekday Mass besides Mass on Sunday.

So, how about it? Let's promise each other that we will avoid all the noise and distractions. Let's spend some time this Advent season with our Lord. I promise it will make your Christmas holiday better than ever. We will behold *"the good news of great joy that will be for all the people. For today in the city of David a savior has been born for you who is Messiah and Lord."* (Luke 2:10, NAB)

Have a blessed Advent.

Reflections: *Look up the word behold in the dictionary. Spend ten minutes today pondering its meaning.*

Chapter 4:

GOD'S GRACE IN DAILY LIFE

Practice Empathy

The observation that "opinions are like belly buttons; everybody has one," is probably truer now than at any time in history. With the advent of social media, anyone can get on Facebook or Twitter and vent on any subject. Hiding behind the anonymity of the internet, people spew venom on anything and everything. Everyone is an expert on everything!

Do we ever take the time to walk in someone else's shoes, to really get to know them, their problems, their frame of reference?

Do we have empathy for others?

We are not talking about sympathy, but empathy. Sympathy is having been there, done that. Empathy requires that we put ourselves in their shoes, even though we have never experienced their situation.

Although the word empathy doesn't appear in the Bible, the Bible has a lot to teach us about empathy:

God, our Creator, empathizes with us.

As a father has compassion on his children, so the LORD has compassion on those who fear him. For he knows how we are formed, remembers that we are dust. — (Psalm 103:13-14, NAB)

Jesus is our model of empathy.

When he disembarked and saw the vast crowd, his heart was moved with pity for them, and he cured their sick. — (Matthew 14:14, NAB)

At the sight of the crowds, his heart was moved with pity for them because they were troubled and abandoned, like sheep without a shepherd. — (Matthew 9:36, NAB)

Jesus showed a great compassion because of his ability to empathize with the crowds. He is sensitive to others' needs and is moved to action.

Empathy (kindness) is a virtue.

Finally, all of you, be of one mind, sympathetic, loving toward one another, compassionate, humble. — (1Peter 3:8, NAB)

Rejoice with those who rejoice, weep with those who weep. — (Romans 12:15, NAB)

Being empathetic and reaching out to others requires us to walk in their shoes.

So, what can we, as Christians, do to be more empathetic?

1. We must **practice active listening**. We've got to really listen to what others are saying, even though we may have never experienced what they are going through. We must work to put ourselves in their place.
2. **Share in others joy and heartbreak.** Are we really happy for their good fortunes? Are we really moved to compassion in their weeping?
3. **We must be mindful in the moment.** Mindfulness requires us not to be quick to judge, but to be non-judgmental and take our time to focus on the emotions, thoughts, and sensations occurring in the present moment. Our opinions can wait!

Before you flame someone's opinion on social media with an all-caps rant, take a minute to put yourself in their shoes. If you do, your response will be mindful and have more empathy.

When you meet strangers, especially those that might be from different cultures, speak different languages, and have different religious beliefs, try being curious. Jesus provides several examples of breaking with the rules of the day and showing empathy, especially with strangers.

You might be surprised that by seeking a higher form of knowledge, you'll not only have more empathy for others, but strengthen your Christian faith, as well. You will better understand the needs of people around you and be more likely to treat the people you care about the way they wish you would treat them. Likewise, you will more clearly understand the perception you create in others with your words and actions.

Let's practice empathy.

Reflections: *How do we practice empathy? Explain the difference between sympathy and empathy? Think of situations where you have been empathetic?*

Reluctant Acceptance

> Do not neglect hospitality, for through it
> some have unknowingly entertained
> angels. — (Hebrews 13:2, NAB)

> Welcome one another, then, as Christ
> welcomed you, for the glory of God. —
> (Romans 15:7, NAB)

> Welcome anyone who is weak in faith,
> but not for disputes over opinions. —
> (Romans 14:1, NAB)

Why are we as a society so reluctant to accept the differences in others?
Why is there a need to judge others?

We shun the disabled or disfigured those with mental health issues or
depression, those of a different faith, race, or sexual orientation. If they
don't look like us, think like us, or act like us, we judge them unworthy.

For many of us, we even have difficulty accepting ourselves, with all of our
flaws and feelings of inadequacy, feelings that we just don't measure up.

If we are truly people of faith, we take solace in knowing that God accepts
us, just as we are, with all of our faults, sins, and misgivings. If we want to
be more like Him, then we need not only to accept ourselves but others as
well. We must let go of our constant judgement of others. We must realize
that sin is sin, and their sin is no greater or worse than ours. Only then, as
Saint Paul reminds us, can we open ourselves to the opportunity to be
entertaining angels!

Do not neglect hospitality, for through it
some have unknowingly entertained
angels. — (Hebrews 13:2, NAB)

When I look back over the past few years, I have had the opportunity to entertain angels:

A disabled jail inmate in a wheel-chair, dying from cancer, gave me insights into living a righteous life that was culled from years of doing just the opposite.

I helped a woman with deep depression to see a light at the end of the tunnel, not by anything I said, but by simply listening.

I learned of the mental anguish of coming to terms with the feelings of being a woman in a man's body from a transsexual acquaintance whose story touched my heart.

I compared the beauty of my Christianity and my love of God and Jesus Christ with a young Zen Buddhist woman as she shared her faith with me. We marveled, not at the differences, but the similarities of our faith experience: gratitude, forgiveness, kindness, and acceptance.

What I have discovered is this; acceptance leads to trust, and trust opens the door to a deeper bond and improved relationships.

No, we don't have to agree on everything we are discussing, and I don't ever have to compromise my Christian beliefs. Everyone is trying to do their best. We are all trying to be the most authentic person we can be.

Do you ever wonder why dogs are considered "man's best friend?" It's simple. They accept people as they are. They don't judge anyone, and they will lick everyone!

This week, let's try to be more accepting of others, let's extend the hospitality of Paul's letter to the Hebrews to those who are different than

123

us. You just might encounter an angel who will change your life and strengthen your faith!

Reflections: *Do you find yourself judging people before you know them? Is love and acceptance the greatest gift? What would you consider to be the greatest gift we can give?*

The Gnat and the Camel

> Woe to you, scribes and Pharisees, you hypocrites. You pay tithes of mint and dill and cumin, and have neglected the weightier things of the law: judgment and mercy and fidelity. [But] these you should have done, without neglecting the others. Blind guides, who strain out the gnat and swallow the camel! — (Matthew 23:23-24, NAB)

Do you sometimes feel that Catholics and Christians get hung up in minutia; that we have become the modern day Pharisees that Jesus admonished? Often, we are so busy being better than others, that we miss the bigger picture. We tend to major in minor subjects!

It seems like righteousness has become a competition.

These "rulebook" Christians are quick to point out the smallest details of why we are doing something wrong and not following the rules. They've got a Bible verse or a reference from the catechism to prove their point. They pay so much attention to these small details that they miss what we are called as Christians to do. They are perfectionists pointing out every imperfection.

If the scribes and Pharisees questioned Jesus about healing people on the Sabbath, talking to a woman at the well, and healing a woman who dared to touch his robe, then, is it any wonder that that some Christians are accused of being narrow-minded, hypocritical, and judgmental?

No one is safe from their criticism, including Pope Francis.

They criticize the pope when he washes the feet of women, children, non-Christians, and even prisoners on Good Friday.

They question his thinking when he says, "Who am I to judge?" when asked about homosexuality, as if he doesn't understand the Bible.

They bash the pope's encyclical, *Laudato Si'*, pointing out that it's alright to disagree because it is just his opinion and that he isn't speaking on faith and morals.

The Pope! They have got a finger pointed at everyone.

If we are to save our church from the decline we have experienced in recent history, we need to quit counting out the smallest seeds and start to look at the things that matter most, the weightier things as pointed out in Matthew's gospel.

We need the world to see the joy in our lives that comes from a deep relationship with Jesus, a joy that comes from humility, forgiveness, and gratitude.

Don't get me wrong, these well-meaning Catholics aren't saying anything that's wrong, just as the Pharisees weren't wrong. They were concerned that a gnat would enter their body, so they strained everything they drank.

However, while they were obsessed with these lesser things, they missed the opportunity to deal with those things that enter the soul, the weightier things of the law, like Justice, Mercy, and Faithfulness.

This is what Jesus is asking us to do:

1. **Promote Justice.** We need to defend the weak among us, the children, unborn, widows, and the poor. We need to stand up for the unemployed, the homeless, the sick, mentally or physically challenged.

    > Make justice your aim: redress the
    > wronged, hear the orphan's plea, defend
    > the widow. — (Isaiah 1:17, NAB)

2. **Show Mercy.** We need to feel the pain and suffering of others. Then, we need to put that compassion to work. We can do that in many ways, from volunteering at the food bank to, visiting those in the hospital, jail, or prison, or praying for God to help them in their need.

3. **Turn our Faith into Faithfulness.** Faith is something we have and faithfulness is putting faith into action.

Let's stop swallowing camels and counting seeds and start focusing on the weightier things. Let people see the joy we have in our service to others, our sense of justice, mercy, and faithfulness.

Then, they will know we are Christians, by our love.

Reflections: Do you find yourself judging people before you know them? What should our approach be to people who don't share our beliefs? What role does mercy play in our Christian lives?

The Power of Hope

> May the God of hope fill you with all joy
> and peace as you trust in him, so that
> you may overflow with hope by the
> power of the Holy Spirit. — (Romans
> 15:13, NAB)

> Into everyone's heart, God has placed a
> search for happiness. Hope responds to
> this desire. It sustains man, frees him
> from discouragement, preserves him
> from selfishness, and leads to happiness
> on earth and in heaven. — (CCC 1818)

Faith, Hope, and Love are the three theological virtues by which we participate in the divine nature of God. Hope is the least understood of these virtues.

Hope is often confused with optimism, of an attitude that things will turn out for the best. Hope is not the result of positive thinking, expecting a good outcome, or denying the reality of a situation.

Hope is much more than that. Hope requires placing our trust in Jesus's promise, and not relying on our own strength, but on the grace of the Holy Spirit. That promise is eternal happiness in the kingdom of Heaven.

Easily said, but tough to do, right?

The woman, demoralized by an abusive, alcoholic husband, knows that it is "wishful thinking" to expect him to turn his life around and be the husband and father he might have been. She realizes that she can't do this herself. She needs the hope that God will provide a way for her, with or without him.

The man diagnosed with brain cancer, undergoes surgery and chemotherapy, only to be told there is nothing more the doctors can do. He knows that a miracle is probably not going to happen, but he has hope that, whatever the outcome, God will provide for his family and he might enjoy the happiness of eternal life and one day they might be together again in heaven.

In the book of Jeremiah 29:11-12, we read, "For I know well the plans I have in mind for you—oracle of the LORD—plans for your welfare and not for woe, so as to give you a future of hope. When you call me, and come and pray to me, I will listen to you." (NAB)

A future of hope, not necessarily the future we were wishing for, might be God's plan for us—a plan for our welfare and not our woe. That hope is unlocked with prayer, a prayer that God's will be done.

Optimism, positive thinking, and a expecting a miraculous outcome are all good things. We should remain positive ourselves and encourage others when they are facing difficult times. Miracles do happen!

In addition, we should have hope in God's plan and give hope to others that God will not forsake us, that He has a plan for us, knows every hair on our head, and gives us the promise of salvation, if we believe in Him.

Our disappointments, marital problems, illnesses, and setbacks are finite. All of these negatives will eventually pass away, but our hope is infinite and God's promise to us is heaven.

There is an Italian proverb that reminds us that "hope is the last thing ever lost." Never lose hope, my friend. We are not of this world, only passing through. Let our hope be in God's promise of eternal life.

Reflections: Do you understand the difference between optimism and hope? How do we stay positive and still hope for God's will? What does it mean to have hope in God's promise?

The Me I'm Meant to Be

For we are his handiwork, created in
Christ Jesus for the good works that
God has prepared in advance, that we
should live in them. — (Ephesians 2:10,
NAB)

So whoever is in Christ is a new creation:
the old things have passed away; behold,
new things have come. — (2 Corinthians
5:17, NAB)

We all wear masks: sometimes to cover our insecurities, sometimes to be
an accepted part of a social group, sometimes as a defense mechanism, and
often to try to ease the task of survival. After a while, we begin to think
that these masks are our reality. We begin to think that we are the person
we portray.

For many of us, something happens in our life that gives us a glimpse,
even for just a moment, of the real person we were meant to be. God is
calling us to be the most authentic version of ourselves.

For example, the star athlete, who spent his high school years making fun
of the frail kid in gym class, may become paralyzed in a horrific automobile
accident. Instead of becoming bitter, he gets a glimpse of the person he
can become and dedicates his life to those in wheel chairs.

The loner, not letting anyone in school know that her family is homeless,
living in her parents' car, gets a glimpse of who she can become. So, she
volunteers at a food pantry and helps found a homeless shelter in her early
30's.

For me, being diagnosed with colon cancer was one turning point in my
life. I realized that many of the things I valued were fleeting. My priorities
were set by a society whose values are not my own.

129

On that very day, God gave me a glimpse of the person I could be. Not being better, holier, smarter, or more loving than anyone else. Just being better than the person I was that day.

Has God ever given you a glimpse or the person you could be? Have you ever thought about the real you, the "me" you were meant to be?

If so, have you begun to move in the direction of a more authentic you?

This past week, at the jail, we spent some time with a young man arrested on a heroin charge. He didn't know much about God, but came to our service just to check things out.

As a young man, he was kicked out of the house, lived homeless in a park, got addicted to heroin, overdosed 15 times, using drugs to mask the pain, depression, and feelings of failure.

Later in our conversation, he talked about having a girlfriend and a job until his arrest, and about getting his GED, and maybe even going to college.

"Awe," I exclaimed. "You have been describing a different person than the one that got you in jail. You have been describing the "me" you might become with God's help. Picture yourself, with a job, a place to live, and becoming a husband and father, who would never let the things that happened to your family. Picture yourself, heroin free, living the 'me' you were meant to be."

There was no miracle conversion that night. I'm not even sure if he made the connection of asking God for help, calling on a "Higher Power" as AA and NA suggest. However, I hope that I helped give him a glimpse of the person he could be.

> Heavenly Father,
> I pray that each person reading this
> might be given a glimpse of the authentic

person they might be. I pray that as a new creation in Jesus, as our old selves pass away, we might, for a moment, behold the new things yet to come. And, I pray that with Your help, I can become the me I was meant to be! In Jesus name, Amen.

Reflections: Have you ever had a glimpse of your best self? How has that changed your approach to life? Do you ever wear a mask to hide your insecurities?

Living with Less

Do not store up for yourselves treasures on earth, where moth and decay destroy, and thieves break in and steal. But store up treasures in heaven, where neither moth nor decay destroys, nor thieves break in and steal. For where your treasure is, there also will your heart be. — (Matthew 6:19-20, NAB)

He said to them in reply, "Whoever has two tunics should share with the person who has none. And whoever has food should do likewise. — (Luke 3:11, NAB)

Let's face it; we live in a society addicted to more. Our homes are 50 percent larger than they were in the 1970's. We covet every new electronic gadget. We supersize our Happy Meals and accumulate more and more stuff.

Americans have bought in to the empty promise of consumerism. We think that more stuff means more happiness and are amazed when we realize that it's just not true.

I have never considered myself a minimalist, but as I get older, I get great joy out of giving away things that I no longer need or use. I have never been a hoarder, my wife Diane has seen to that. As a decorator, she is always decluttering our home and our lives.

At least twice a year, she goes through our home with a fine-tooth comb and makes trips to St. Vincent DePaul, Marian's Closet, Haven of Rest, Habitat for Humanity and other local organizations that help those in need, with wonderful items we no longer need.

> Find out how much God has given you
> and from it take what you need; the
> remainder is needed by others. — (Saint
> Augustine)

As we give away furniture, clothing, and housewares, an interesting thing happens. We realize that in addition to helping someone else, we didn't need these possessions in the first place.

Instead of chasing stuff, we are free to chase gratitude and generosity, realizing that everything we have and give is a gift from God.

Instead of investing in stuff, we are free to invest in our spiritual growth and our relationships with family and friends.

As it says in Matthew's gospel, "Do not store up for yourselves treasures on earth, where moth and decay destroy, and thieves break in and steal. But store up treasures in heaven, where neither moth nor decay destroys, nor thieves break in and steal. For where your treasure is, there also will your heart be" (6:19-21, NAB)

Here is the best part: as we declutter and live with less, we find ourselves desiring less. We realize that desiring less is more valuable that owning less! It's liberating!

The same is true for money. How we use money is one of the greatest spiritual indicators. Do we take from our excess and put our money to work where it will do the most good. Do we support those charities and ministries that we identify with?

As the old saying goes, money and possessions are lousy lovers. In the book of Ecclesiastes (5:10-15, NAB) we learn what money and possessions can't buy: contentment, friendship, peace of mind, security, and life after death.

> He said to them in reply, "Whoever has two tunics should share with the person who has none. And whoever has food should do likewise. —— (Luke 3:11, NAB)

Why not give it a try. There is no time like the present to get started. Start small. Your home, garage, office, or attic might contain items that can help a young family just getting started have a couch, chair, or table that you are no longer using. Those old, but still good, pots and pans you put in the basement when you got the new ones, would be a great starter set for someone going off to college. The boxes of hardly worn baby clothes in the attic might help a struggling single mother, providing her with beautiful outfits that she could never afford. The old lawn mower sitting in the back of the garage might help a new homeowner forced to choose between purchasing a new one or feeding his family.

I promise you'll not only feel good as you live the life that Jesus asks of you, but happiness and joy will also follow. You will be living the Christian lifestyle.

Let's get started!

Reflections: *Do you find yourself accumulating stuff that you don't really need? Is it difficult for you to donate things that you are no longer using? Do you find yourself attached to things and not people?*

A God Appointment

> Again I say to you, it is easier for a camel
> to pass through the eye of a needle than
> for one who is rich to enter the kingdom
> of God. — (Matthew 19:24, NAB)

Today I had a God appointment. This morning as I was reading the morning office, I had a strong feeling that I should forego morning Mass and go at noontime at St. Bernard's, an inner-city church where I work.

Why would I do that? I was awake and had plenty of time to make it to morning Mass. I decided the urging must be coming from the Holy Spirit that God wanted me at noon Mass for a reason. It was a God appointment.

As I entered the church, I immediately spotted Keith sitting where I usually sit whenever I attend Mass there. I had met Keith a few years earlier. At the time, he was homeless. We kept in touch, seeing each other from time to time.

As we made eye contact, he smiled a huge smile. Keith is a slight black man with a deep love of God. As I made my way to the row and took a seat next to him, I noticed that he was praying the rosary, so I didn't disturb him.

I wondered if seeing Keith was the God appointment. Was I there to help Keith? Perhaps he was homeless again or maybe he needed some money for food? Maybe God was calling me to minister to Keith?

After Mass, we talked for nearly half an hour. Keith had quit his job after being continuously screamed at and made to feel worthless by two other employees. He wondered if he could find another. God had given Keith a hard life.

Why would our Lord put so many obstacles in his way? Why couldn't Keith get a break?

I wondered why my life has been so blessed and easy.

I thought back to the gospel reading we had heard just a few minutes earlier, about rich people having a harder time getting into heaven.

Keith had the answer. He said, "God has given me a hard life so I will appreciate things. My room has no running water, so I appreciate water, soap, and shampoo. I appreciate a shower and a roll of toilet paper. I realize that everything I have is a gift from God. I am so grateful!"

Wow, I will never look at a bar of soap or a roll of toilet paper the same way again!

What do I appreciate? What am I grateful for?" We spend so much time worrying about the things we want that we fail to appreciate the things we already have.

135

Debbie isn't satisfied with her 5 series BMW. She really wanted the 7 series. Keith appreciates soap.

Tom wanted the sixty-inch flat-panel television but could only afford the forty-seven inch. He finds it hard to appreciate the one he has. Keith is grateful for a roll of toilet paper.

Ryan finds it hard to love his forty-foot Sea Ray boat in a harbor of fifty-foot-plus yachts. Keith appreciates taking a shower.

No wonder Jesus warned about the difficulty of the rich entering heaven. It's about gratitude, understanding that everything we have is from God. It's about appreciating little things.

I am certainly not rich, but I have a job, a home with running water, and soap and toilet paper. I need to take a minute to be grateful for these things.

If you are not grateful for the things you have, what makes you think you will be grateful for the things you want?

Are you grateful for little things? If you are, it will certainly make getting into heaven easier.

I attended Mass today expecting that God would use me to minister to someone, and instead Keith was ministering to me.

As we parted, I gave him some money for gasoline for his truck and food to get by and the promise that I would keep him in my prayers. He promised to pray for me as well.

As it turned out God had a better plan. He always does, if we just open ourselves to listening to Him. He might just have a God appointment waiting for you.

Reflections: Do you find yourself thinking about what you want and forget being thankful for what you already have? What role does gratitude play in your everyday life? Have you ever had a God appointment?

Sin—what's Your Excuse?

> If your hand or foot causes you to sin,
> cut it off and throw it away. It is better
> for you to enter into life maimed or
> crippled than with two hands or two feet
> to be thrown into eternal fire. And if
> your eye causes you to sin, tear it out and
> throw it away. It is better for you to
> enter into life with one eye than with two
> eyes to be thrown into fiery Gehenna. —
> (Matthew -18:8-9, NAB)

Excuses, we all make them. Sometimes they are harmless, other times they can be life-changing, shameful, or dishonest.

We put off yearly medical exams, mammograms, colonoscopies, and dental exams, always finding something else in our lives more important. Sometimes we put them off so long that a problem that could have been diagnosed early is out of control. We are embarrassed that our excuses caused us to put our health at risk.

We want to get together with an old friend in a nearby city, but, something is always more important and we make lame excuses why we can't visit.

137

Years go by, our friend passes away, and we forever regret that we never made seeing them a priority.

A disagreement results in family members taking sides. Years pass without them speaking to one another, estranged from the people that they should love the most. Years later, they can't even remember the reason for the split. They want to reconcile, but old wounds make for too many excuses. Only a family tragedy brings them together.

Yes, excuses are powerful life-changing road-blocks to our happiness.

The same holds true for sin. Each of us is born with an understanding of right and wrong. It's imprinted on our DNA. Nevertheless, we still sin, even while knowing that it is wrong. We have excuses for every sin!

"It's in my background."

"I was brought up that way."

"Everyone is doing it."

"Someone hurt me; I was falsely accused!"

Don't feel bad. The Bible is full of people making excuses! Adam and Eve had an excuse. So did Cain, and, Noah's people. Even Satan made excuses.

So, how do we begin to put these excuses aside and declare, *No More Excuses* for sin? How do we take ownership of our sins and eliminate the excuses for continuing to commit the same ones?

First, we must recognize the temptation and admit our weakness in dealing with it. Then, pray for the grace to overcome the temptation and resist it.

Here are a few actions that we can take to do this;

1. **Pray for the grace to resist the temptation.** Most people commit the same sins over and over again. Prayer is a powerful defense against sin.
2. **Avoid sinful places and people.** My dad used to say, "You become who you hang out with." If you go places where you are flirting with sin or hang out with people who lead you to sin, you will find resisting difficult.
3. **Stop blaming others or the situation.** The devil didn't make you do it and neither did anyone else. You are singularly responsible for your actions and no self-justification applies.
4. **Stop procrastinating.** I'll start the new diet next week, or this fall I'll get back to the gym. We simply put off taking action. It is simply just another excuse. It's the same with sin. If you want to stop sinning, start now!

In Matthew 18, Jesus uses the technique of amplification and exaggeration, customary of the times, to make a point of the power and seriousness of sin. We don't need to start cutting off limbs and plucking out our eyes, but we do need to make the pledge of "no more excuses!"

Reflections: What are your excuses for sin? Do you find yourself committing the same sin over and over? What change can you make to help you prevent sin?

Authentic People

Do not conform yourselves to this age
but be transformed by the renewal of
your mind, that you may discern what is
the will of God, what is good and
pleasing and perfect. — (Romans 12:2,
NAB)

But the Lord said to Samuel: Do not
judge from his appearance or from his
lofty stature, because I have rejected him.
God does not see as a mortal, who sees
the appearance. The Lord looks into the
heart. —— (1 Samuel 16:7, NAB,
Emphasis added)

We all know authentic people. We are attracted to them. They exude kindness and compassion, they don't judge, they are trustworthy, passionate, helpful and genuine.

Yet, in a world where we celebrate narcissistic, self-centered, egotistical behavior, why aren't more people seeking their authentic self? The television schedule is full of programs celebrating the Kardashian's, Real Housewives, and self-centered musical artists who by default become today's role models for our youth. We are more concerned with the value of our possessions than the value of our souls.

Authenticity is a word that gets used often in articles, on social media, and in conversations. But what is it? And, what defines an authentic person? What makes authentic people different?

Here are ten things that authentic people do differently:

1. **Authentic people express their opinions and feelings**. They never fake their response to "fit in" with the crowd. They don't

take it personally if people disagree, but speak the truth unapologetically. This is particularly true when discussing their faith.

2. **They are driven internally not externally.** Really authentic people listen to their inner-voice; they follow their heart, seek their purpose in life and choose their own career. They never allow external others to influence their decisions. Prayer and meditation guide their path.

3. **They have good self-esteem** and appreciate themselves and their accomplishments, but they keep their self-esteem at a healthy level, never becoming self-centered and narcissistic. They realize that everything they have is a gift from God to use in a positive way. They have unique traits and rituals like daily prayer, Mass attendance, meditation, praying the rosary, all requiring some self-discipline.

4. **They choose experiences over things.** Authentic people love to experience life and share experiences with family and friends. They would rather share "Kodak moments" with those they love, than buying themselves a bigger house, newer car, or the latest iPhone.

5. **They are non-judgmental and always kind.** Authentic people understand that we are all different and come from different traditions and cultures. They celebrate these differences without ever compromising their own deeply held beliefs. When someone attacks their beliefs, they don't take things personally or react with anger or aggression.

6. **Authentic people make the most of bad situations**. They trust God completely and are free of fear. Understanding that suffering is part of life, they seek to learn from every bad situation, without fear of failure and always trusting in the Lord's plan for their lives.

7. **They support others and always wish them success**. Authentic people love and rejoice in the success of others. They are never jealous when a friend gets a promotion, wins a game, or receives an honor. They wish no one harm.

8. **Authentic people avoid negative people**. They find themselves being attracted to upbeat positive people. When an authentic

person is in a crowd of gossipers, they kindly and quickly remove themselves from the situations. Negative people drain energy from a room, and an authentic person intuitively recognizes this quickly and simply leaves.

9. **They seek the soul and not the person**. Authentic people don't care how you dress, what kind of car you drive, or the size of your bank account. They realize that some of the greatest wisdom they have ever received has come from ordinary people with extraordinary stories and beautiful souls.

10. **Authentic people hunger for the truth**. They are seekers, always looking for the truth. They read the Bible and other great books, attend seminars and workshops, and classes. They realize that life lessons are rarely learned in school, but in a life-long pursuit of truth and wisdom.

Imagine if we all worked on improving our lives by adopting and developing these common traits. We need a strong desire to be the most authentic version of ourselves. With God's help we can become the "me" we were meant to be!

Reflections: *Who is the most authentic person you know? Do you find that people often try to be someone they aren't? How about you?*

Christians Include; Pharisees Exclude

The Christian includes, he does not close the door to anyone, even if this provokes resistance. He who excludes, because he believes himself to be better, generates

conflicts and divisions, and does not
consider the fact that "we shall all stand
before the judgment seat of God. —
(Pope Francis, 2015)

Exclusion was popular in Jesus's time. The Pharisees, a popular Jewish renewal movement, looked down on the majority of Jews as unclean masses, the "people of the land." Their exclusionism was often linked with their sense of piety.

Is it any wonder, then, that the Pharisees had problems with Jesus? Jesus included tax collectors and sinners, lepers and women among his followers. These common sinners were drawn to Jesus, because he was inclusive. Keep in mind that Jesus never accepted their sin, but, he knew that beating them over the head with the law wasn't the best way to get them to lead a more righteous life.

Those who are judgmental drive people away. They consider themselves better than others and generate conflict and division. They risk the judgement of God. Pope Francis reminds us that Christ unites and includes "all men in salvation." We should never close the door of our Christian faith to anyone.

Throughout all of salvation history there have always been those who close the door on anyone who doesn't think, act, and judge as they do. Human nature hasn't changed; people still feel superior to those they exclude.

What about today? Are there modern-day Pharisees? Are their people so concerned with the rule book that they exclude anyone who doesn't believe as they do?

The answer is yes!

In their zeal for the faith, they fail to realize that not everyone is at the same point in their personal faith journey. Many have never heard the message of forgiveness, redemption, and salvation through Jesus. If they are driven away, they will never have the opportunity to share the faith. Jesus accepted people just as they were, never accepting their sin, but always accepting them. The more they were drawn to Him, the more they moved away from their sin.

Ask a non-Christian or young person their impression of Christians and they will say that Christians are judgmental, hypocritical, and insensitive. That doesn't sound like people that are supposed to be Christ to the world. In fact, it sounds un-Christian! When the modern-day Pharisees read this, they'll find a myriad of excuses why their critic's' impressions are incorrect.

Yet, that is the reality. Church attendance continues to decline each year! Like the Pharisees, they believe that adherence to their narrow interpretation of the law is the solution rather that the cause of the decline.

As Pope Francis continues to remind us, the Christian "includes," the Pharisee "excludes." That is why he has talked of a more inclusive church, one that gets its hands dirty, serving the poor, marginalized, and excluded "people of the land."

What can we do to be more inclusive without compromising our faith? How can we avoid the trap of becoming a modern-day Pharisee and be more Christ-like?

1. **Let's shine the light of Christ** to draw people to him, not drive them away. People are drawn to sincerity, sensitivity, respect, and gentleness. If we meet people where they are in their faith journey with respect and sincerity, we will shine the light of Jesus on them. We can't ask people to behave before they believe! As we are reminded in 2 Corinthians 4:6, "For God who said, "Let light shine out of darkness,"" has shone in our hearts to bring to light the knowledge of the glory of God on the face of [Jesus] Christ." (NAB)

2. **Let's allow the Holy Spirit to work in us**. In Galatians, we learn of the fruits of the Holy Spirit: love, joy, peace, forbearance, kindness, goodness, faithfulness, gentleness, and self-control.

Most Christians like the idea of the virtues, but not necessarily the practice of them! We need to filter our actions through the virtues.

3. **Let's share the truth of the faith with them in love.** People need truth and love! We need to lead with love. In Ephesians 4:15, we read, "Rather, living the truth in love, we should grow in every way into him who is the head." (NAB)

4. **Let's pray for them.** I don't have to agree with anyone to pray that the Lord touches them in a special way and opens them to the truth of our Christian faith. Let's pray for those who are lost, rather that judge them.

Let's strive to act as true Christians who "include," rather than fall into the role of modern-day Pharisees who "exclude." Let's not lose the opportunity to share our beautiful Christian faith with love.

Reflections: Have you ever been turned off by a turned-on Christian? Do you find yourself being judgmental, especially with strangers? With the people you love? Are young people correct when they accuse Christians of being judgmental?

Because I'm Entitled

You covet but do not possess. You kill and envy but you cannot obtain; you fight and wage war. You do not possess because you do not ask. You ask but do not receive, because you ask wrongly to spend it on your passions. — (James 4:2-3, NAB)

We read a lot these days about entitlement, about those self-centered narcissists that think of themselves as the center of the universe. Millennials are often depicted as the entitlement generation, with their baby boomer parents to blame. However, entitlement stretches across several generations. We baby boomers and Gen Xers can be just as guilty. We have all experienced self-centered, entitled narcissists. If the universe doesn't meet every need and desire then all hell breaks loose.

More and more people are worried about the sense of entitlement that has crept into their homes, families, and neighborhoods.

What are the signs and symptoms of entitlement? How can we know if our children, spouses, siblings, or even we ourselves are guilty of a sense of entitlement?

1. We live in an angry world. If things don't go our way we feel like there has to be someone to blame. Road rage, cop killings, and rioting fans react with anger if things don't go their way.
2. If there is something that they want and don't get, they become resentful. They never appreciate what they have and resent every desire that isn't fulfilled. They also resent anyone who gets in their way.
3. A sense of entitlement will make people cynical about everything. We have a generation of cynics, with a negative, jaded opinion on every subject.
4. The narcissistic person not only wants everything they desire, they want it now! They become impatient having to wait for anything.
5. Entitlement and gratitude are opposites. Instead of being grateful for what they have, an entitled person feels ingratitude for what they want and don't yet have.

Do you recognize any of these emotions in your family and friends? Are you guilty of any of these emotions yourself?

What are we, as Christians, to do to overcome these emotions?

We need to control our anger. If we knew what was going on with the person in the other car or ahead of us at the checkout, or blocking the sidewalk, we might be more forgiving. We need to put others' needs ahead of our own.

We need to put life into perspective. Young people often want right now what their parents worked a lifetime to achieve. That beautiful home came after twenty-five years of hard work. It's wonderful to have goals in life, but they rarely happen until we have put in the time and effort to achieve them.

We need patience. We need to understand that sometimes we must delay gratification until a later time. We might want to win the championship, but we have to keep in mind that life is a marathon and not a sprint. There will be setbacks. If we are patient, gratification is much sweeter.

We need to be grateful. When we have a realistic view of the big picture, we can really be grateful for what we have. If we can't appreciate what we already have, then how can we ever appreciate what we desire once we get it?

Don't let entitlement creep into your lives or the lives of your loved ones. Only through self-awareness can we find hope and optimism. Forgiveness, patience, perspective, and gratitude are the antidote to cure an entitled generation.

Reflections: *How should you react to the angry people around you? Do you notice entitlement in your family or among your friends? Are you guilty of feeling a sense of entitlement?*

Are You the One?

When John heard in prison of the works
of the Messiah, he sent his disciples to
him with this question, "Are you the one
who is to come, or should we look for
another?" — (Matthew 11:2-3, NAB)

Jesus said to him, 'If you can!'
Everything is possible to one who has
faith. Then the boy's father cried out, "I
do believe, help my unbelief!" — (Mark
9:23-24, NAB)

So he got up and went back to his father.
While he was still a long way off, his
father caught sight of him, and was filled
with compassion. He ran to his son,
embraced him and kissed him. — (Luke
15:20, NAB)

Doubts; we have them at times. As Christians, we are embarrassed by our
doubt. Is the story of Jesus true? Did he really die for my sins?

- Noah had doubts when he built the Ark.
- Abraham had doubts when he offered to sacrifice his son Isaac.
- Moses had doubts when he led his people across the Red Sea.
- David had doubts when he faced Goliath.

We know that Blessed Saint Mother Teresa had doubts, as she wrote about
her "dark night of the soul."

Even John the Baptist, arguably the greatest prophet of the Bible, asked
our Lord, "Are you the one who is to come?"

In Matthew 11:11, Jesus said that "among those born of women there has been none greater than John the Baptist," yet, as John rotted away in prison, even he had doubts. (NAB)

As we prepare for the coming of Jesus during Advent, we can use this time to read, study, talk to friends who have a strong faith, confess our sins, and recommit ourselves to living a Christ-like life.

What most people fail to realize is that doubt is not the opposite of faith; disbelief is. Doubt can actually build our faith and be the catalyst for spiritual growth.

Doubt is not sinful and unforgivable. God is big enough to handle all of our questions if we are moving in the direction of faith. It does not indicate a lack of faith, but a desire to have our faith grow.

Here are a few things to remember:

God is kind and merciful. He is patient with us and loves us more than we know. Like the father of the prodigal son, all we need to do is move in his direction and He will rush to greet us!

Our struggles bring new growth in faith. If we are totally free of doubt, we are probably already in Heaven! As long as we are moving in the direction of light and not darkness, then; even in our doubt, we are moving closer to God.

In prayer, it's OK to admit our doubt and tell God how we feel. We can ask God to "help my unbelief." God will never give up on us. In His compassion and patience, He will wait for us and bless our searching.

Advent is a time to discover a closer and more intimate relationship with our Lord, to confront our doubts and turn them into a stronger, more vibrant faith. Then, we can answer John the Baptist's question, "Are you the one?"

On Christmas morning, we can answer with a resounding *yes*! Jesus, the One, has come into the world, our Savior, born of a virgin in Bethlehem.

Halleluiah!

Reflections: *Do you think your doubt is a lack of faith? Do you think doubt can actually lead to a greater faith? What will you be doing during Advent to grow your faith?*

Cast Your Nets

As he passed by the Sea of Galilee, he saw Simon and his brother Andrew casting their nets into the sea; they were fishermen. Jesus said to them, "Come after me, and I will make you fishers of men." Then they abandoned their nets and followed him. He walked along a little farther and saw James, the son of Zebedee, and his brother John. They too were in a boat mending their nets. Then he called them. So they left their father Zebedee in the boat along with the hired men and followed him. — (Mark 1:16-20, NAB)

Andrew, the brother of Simon Peter, was one of the two who heard John and followed Jesus. He first found his own brother Simon and told him, "We have found the Messiah" Then he brought him to Jesus. Jesus looked at him and said, "You are Simon the son of John; you will be called Cephas (Peter)" — (John 1 40-42, NAB)

Those who accepted his message were baptized, and about three thousand persons were added that day. — (Act 2:41, NAB)

Do you ever feel like your life is one big assembly line? You do the same things every day at the same time. Just as in the movie *"Groundhog's Day,"* we wake and shower, have breakfast and drive to work, sit at the same desk, do the same tasks, and return home to the same easy chair. Life becomes a comfortable rut.

I imagine it was the same for Simon and Andrew and James and John. Every day they would go to the same lake, cast their nets, bring in the fish, and mend their nets, only to do it again the next day. They were fishermen, and life became a comfortable rut, casting their nets over and over again.

So, when Jesus approached them, they were busy earning a living, doing what they did best, what they were trained to do, a life that had become a comfortable rut.

But, when Jesus said, *"Come follow me!"* Simon and Andrew immediately abandoned their nets and followed Jesus, who promised to make them fishers of men.

The same was true for James and John. They left behind their livelihood, their father, Zebedee and their crew to follow Jesus.

Why would they do this? They weren't poor; they had good jobs and were making a good living as fishermen. They gave up everything they had to follow Jesus.

Are we willing to do the same?

As you cast the nets of your daily routine, is Jesus calling you to follow him? Is he asking you to become a fisher of men?

We know from the gospels that Andrew had been searching for God and a meaning to his life. The disciple, John the Baptist, introduced Andrew to Jesus.

They were not concerned with what they gave up, but what they were to gain. Each of them was following a deep desire for God in their lives. Nothing that Jesus asked of them was in conflict with this deep desire.

They truly did become fishers of men. In Acts 2, we read that Simon Peter brought three-thousand people into the faith in one day.

Isn't that what everyone desires in their life—a relationship with God?

Is our Lord calling you to serve Him? Is He asking you to become a fisher of men? Are you willing to share your faith with family, friends, co-workers, and even strangers? Good question, right?

For some of us, the call is deep and loud! Entering the priesthood, religious life, or full-time ministry might be the message. For others, it might be simply to get involved with an apostolate. Working with the poor and homeless, jail ministry, teaching religious education, or any of a huge number of possible directions can be your way to "cast your net" for the glory of God.

Following Jesus goes beyond Sunday Mass and being a good person. It requires that we use our talents and abilities, whatever they may be, to help others in their search for God.

Take a moment this week to reflect on Jesus's call. When Jesus asks that you, "come follow me," don't think about what you might have to give up, but what you have to gain in the Kingdom of God. Then, don't hesitate; the apostles didn't! Decide to respond to that deep desire for God in your life.

Imagine a world where all Christians were "casting their nets" and becoming fishers of men.

Reflections: *Are you willing to cast your nets and become a fisher of men? What can you gain by not hesitating to follow Jesus? How do you get out of the rut and become a true disciple?*

Don't Buy Green Bananas

> For he says: "In an acceptable time I heard you, and on the day of salvation I helped you." Behold, **now** is a very acceptable time; behold, **now** is the day of salvation. — (2 Corinthians 6:2, NAB, Emphasis added.)

There is a story of a financial advisor who sat down with an 85-year-old man to go over his investments. He suggested a few stocks that he thought would give the elderly man a quick return. Then, the broker suggested that he look at some safer, long-term investments.

"Long-term investments?" the old man exclaimed. "I don't even buy green bananas!"

There are many stories with the same theme attributed to everyone from Ann Landers to Senator Sam Nunn. Even country artist Jake Owen has a song about an older fishing buddy whose boat was named "Green Bananas." In every case, the message is clear: life is too short to wait for the things you want.

Just before Christmas, Diane and I attended the funerals or calling hours for six friends and relatives in one week. One was my brother-in-law, who was also a very close friend. Another was only 41 and died in his sleep. Each passing drove home the point that life is too short to wait to do the things we need or even want to do. We can't wait for things to be perfect for us to act. Whether it's a new job, a move to another city, a trip to Europe, or to simply visit a friend we haven't seen in years, the time to do it is now!

For many years, my mom had planned a trip to Italy. It was her life-long dream. She had her passport ready and on several occasions had booked the trip only to have something happen to cause her to cancel her plans. It was her dream until the day she died. She never made the trip.

Many years later, Diane and I were celebrated our 25th wedding anniversary with a trip to Italy. I brought my mom's passport and had it stamped whenever we passed through customs. In every church we visited, we lit a candle for her, and I vowed never to put off meaningful things, and that included my faith.

Don't wait to say, "I love you."
Don't wait to say, "I'm sorry."
Don't wait to forgive.
Don't wait to strengthen your relationship with Jesus.

I hear it all the time.

"I'll go back to church when I get married or when we have kids."
"I'll get married when I lose twenty pounds."
"I'll take that vacation with my family when I pay off the car."

Before we get around to it, something unforeseen happens. An accident, illness, job loss, bankruptcy, or death of a loved one will remind us that life is precious and we may never get the chance to do the things we know we must do, unless we do them now!

The same is true with our faith?

What is God calling you to do? Is He asking you to reconcile with a loved one, forgive someone that has hurt you in the past, or ask forgiveness for something you said that you regret?

Why are you hesitating? Are you guilty of buying green bananas, expecting them to ripen later? Are you simply procrastinating? Or, do you think that it can wait?

It is said that Satan's greatest lie is that you have plenty of time to get right with God.

Don't wait for the right time, place, or circumstances. Life is short; there is no time for hesitation, procrastination, excuses, or green bananas!

You can do it!

Reflections: *Have you ever put off something thinking that you would have time later? Have you ever been guilty of putting off God, thinking you can get to Him later? Has experiencing the death of a loved one prompted you to think about taking action on something you previously put off? What things?*

Iron Sharpens Iron

Iron is sharpened by iron; one person sharpens another. — (Proverbs 27:17, NAB)

We are fools on Christ's account, but you are wise in Christ; we are weak, but you are strong; you are held in honor, but we in disrepute. — (1 Corinthians 4:10, NAB)

Indeed, the word of God is living and effective, sharper than any two-edged sword, penetrating even between soul and spirit, joints and marrow, and able to discern reflections and thoughts of the heart. — (Hebrews 4:12, NAB)

Yesterday, as I sat at daily Mass, it occurred to me that I was surrounded by a dozen male friends. We have made a habit of sitting together at daily Mass and going to breakfast or out for coffee a few times each week. We even have a name for our group, "Fools for Christ," taken from 1Corinthians.

We are all different in many ways. Some are employed, some unemployed, some retired. We work in a variety of fields from insurance to taxes, communications to medicine, and pharmaceuticals to construction. We all have different interests and ministries. Some are involved in healing ministry. Some serve the homeless, others in Legion of Mary, St. Vincent DePaul, and Catholic radio.

Yet, we all have one thing in common, our love for Christ and his church.

Just as iron sharpens iron, we sharpen each other!

Unless you haven't been paying attention, we have a crisis in Christianity. Fewer and fewer people are attending Mass and Sunday services. Church attendance has fallen from over 80 percent in 1950 to just over 20 percent today. A disproportionate share of that decline is among men.

More and more, men are attempting to navigate the tough problems of life alone. They have no one to share their frustrations with, no one to go to for advice, no one to hold them accountable.

God never intended man to go it alone. We need friends.

A dull knife is still a knife, but when sharpened, it is sharper, brighter, and fit for use. The same is true for men. A man going it alone is still a man, but he is dull, sad, and inactive, and sometimes confused and paralyzed. Friendship is like the sharpening instrument. It sharpens our thinking, refreshes our direction, revives our love of God, and clarifies our actions.

Two of the same knives can't sharpen each other. It takes a different kind of iron to sharpen them. The fact that my friends are all different gives each of us the opportunity to sharpen others. We all have our strengths and weaknesses, and I have learned something different from each of them.

Spending time together gives us a chance to pray, encourage, exhort, admonish, and help each other. Sharing the word of God is like that "two-edged" sword that strengthens each of us.

If you are struggling and going it alone, you should try finding a group of men you can join. It was easy back in college, but those guys are gone. You need to find some new friends. Here are a couple of suggestions:

1. **Seek out a men's group at church**. Often, you can join a Bible study, men's prayer group, or service project that will help introduce you to some new people. Our "Fools for Christ" group came about from the merging of several other groups that disbanded.

157

2. **Find or start your own breakfast or lunch group**. Years ago, when I lived in Atlanta, we had a group of guys that met for lunch on Wednesdays. Not all of us could make every lunch, but there was always a few guys each week that could help provide a mid-week lift in faith.
3. **Find men with a common interest** at work, school, or on a team, and get together away from that activity. Often guys are just waiting for someone to ask. Don't be afraid to take that first step.

God didn't intend for us to go it alone. We need male friends to help us on our life journey. We need men to help rebuild the church, but to do that we've got to be involved, engaged and intentional about your Christian faith.

You can do this, and I promise that you will enjoy a more confident and rewarding life with your own "fools for Christ." Remember, iron sharpens iron and people sharpen people. Until then, I'll be praying for you.

Reflections: *Do you have a group of friends that can keep you connected to Christ? Do you have male friends that can keep you accountable? Do you have male friends that you can go to for advice and prayer?*

Coping with Change

Do not conform yourselves to this age
but be transformed (changed) by the
renewal of your mind, that you may
discern what is the will of God, what is

good and pleasing and perfect. —
(Romans 12:2, NAB)

Be strong and steadfast; have no fear or
dread of them, for it is the LORD, your
God, who marches with you; he will
never fail you or forsake you. —
(Deuteronomy 31:6, NAB)

It is said that the only thing certain in life is that things will change. It's true. Change is something we all resist, dislike, and wish would never happen. It brings stress, discomfort, and makes us feel that we have lost control.

The loss of a loved one or dear friend—brings about a change that is totally out of our control. A job loss, financial loss, a move to a new town or college, can add to our stress.

Stress is something we really don't like. A friend of mine always says, "The only people that like change are wet babies!" Funny, but true!

So, how do we cope with change? How do we react to things that are totally out of our control? What promises does our Lord make about dealing with the changes in our lives?

It is important to understand that God is in control, not us. Understand that we didn't do anything wrong to be facing these changes. God won't change our circumstances, but He will sustain us and give us the tools necessary to get us through them.

It is important to acknowledge that change is inevitable. Our lives are always changing in some small way, but the big ones require us to face our feelings, manage our stress, and try to understand this unwanted change.

Here are a few things to keep in mind:

1. **God never changes and neither does His love.** Jesus is the same yesterday, today, and forever. Be strong. Remember that God will always be there for you, won't abandon you, and has your back.
2. **God is with you.** Sometimes following the loss of a loved one, we feel that God has abandoned us, or that we may have done something wrong in our lives that caused God to punish us. Nothing could be further from the truth. God is waiting for us, with open arms to help us and guide us through the stress and pain. Don't fear; turn to our Lord in prayer and he will give you the tools to cope.
3. **God will guide our way.** Change takes time. It's a process, and prayer will help us get the answers. We need to acknowledge the change and our feelings. We need to ask our Lord to help us and guide us. Through prayer, we can face our feelings, be grateful, and set goals for moving forward with our lives.

There is an ancient quote from Socrates that says, "the secret of change is to focus all of your energy, not on fighting the old, but on building the new." (Socrates) Let's pray that God will help us concentrate on what's ahead for our lives. It's not that we can or want to forget the past but rather we need to re-frame our thinking about the future.

Change means growing and learning. We realize that our lives will change over time, and occasionally there are major changes that will challenge us

Let the change bring us closer to our Lord, closer to the person we are meant to be, closer to God's promise to always be with us, never abandon us, and to lead us to everlasting life.

That is my prayer for you, my friend.

Reflections: *Have you had a problem coping with change? Do you ever feel as if God abandoned you? In times of trouble, do you move closer to God or push yourself away?*

Be the One

> Those who seek the good seek favor, but
> those who pursue evil will have evil
> come upon them. — (Proverbs 11:27,
> NAB)

> Who is the man who delights in life, who
> loves to see the good days? Keep your
> tongue from evil, your lips from
> speaking lies. Turn from evil and do
> good; seek peace and pursue it. ——
> (Psalm 34:13-15, NAB)

In the book of Proverbs we are offered two ways to live our lives. We can
be seekers of good or pursuers of evil. We can have a positive attitude
building people up, or a negative one tearing people down.

Do you know someone who is always spreading the dirt about relatives,
friends, or people at work? It seems that they never have a nice thing to
say about anyone. Have you found that their negativity rubs off on you?
Does it steal your energy? I have.

Or, are you the one spreading negative thoughts and don't even know it?
Are you willingly participating in the daily gossip to be accepted as part of
the crowd?

Lent is a great time to ask ourselves if we are willingly or even unwillingly
adding to the negativity in our lives. Are we critical and negative, bitter and
envious of others? Are we hurtful and selfish? If so, Proverbs warns us, we
will have sad, painful, and troubled lives.

Have you ever heard the saying *"what goes around comes around?"* If you
associate with negative people, you will become negative. Hang out with
complainers, you will be a complainer. Bitter, envious, selfish friends will

161

make you a bitter, envious, and selfish person. You will never make positive changes in your life if you surround yourself with negative people.

Pope Francis in his Ash Wednesday message said that if we want to give up something for Lent, we should give up indifference to our neighbor. Let's try to seek the gold in others and spread positive energy. Let's do it not only during Lent, but every day.

> Indifference to our neighbor and to God also represents a real temptation for us Christians. Each year during Lent we need to hear once more the voice of the prophets who cry out and trouble our conscience. — (Pope Francis, 2013)

What can we do to heighten the awareness of our surroundings and seek the gold in others, rather than digging up the dirt?

1. **Avoid negative people!** Years ago, whenever I approached people who were gossiping or spreading negativity, I walked away. I didn't want their negativity to rub off on my positive attitude. I joked that I was allergic to them.
2. **Look for solutions!** Negative people are never looking for solutions, never looking for ways to make things better. If they did, they would have nothing to complain about and would have to find the next thing to complain about.
3. **Optimism is a happiness magnet!** Finding positive people to associate with, people looking to build people up, find solutions, and interested in personal growth, will add to your happiness.
4. **Be the Yes, but...person.** When people are spreading rumors about someone, I will often interrupt them with a yes...but, and then I will share a positive thought about the person being targeted.

"That may be true, BUT when I was in the hospital, she was the first person to visit me."

"Yes, BUT he really went out of his way to help get that project completed on time."

You get the idea, right? Remember, if they are talking behind someone's back when they aren't there, they are talking about you behind your back too!

Let's start right now, during Lent, to find the gold in others, to be optimistic and positive. Let's shed the negative behavior and avoid letting negative people steal our joy. Let's bring a new energy to all that we do, and seek God's favor not just during Lent but every day of our lives.

Are you with me? We can do this, my friend.

Reflections: How do you rid yourself of negativity? Do you seek opportunities to praise? Have you ever been involved in spreading rumors? Ever get caught? How did that make you feel?

A Still, Small Voice

For man has in his heart a law inscribed
by God. . . . His conscience is man's
most secret core and his sanctuary.
There he is alone with God whose voice
echoes in his depths. — (CCC 1776)

Faced with a moral choice, conscience
can make either a right judgment in
accordance with reason and the divine

law or, on the contrary, an erroneous
judgment that departs from them. —
(CCC 1799)

We often read of that still, small voice that is in each of us. It is a voice
guiding our path, discerning right from wrong, helping us make decisions
that will forever be part of our lives.

It is our moral conscience, formed over time, based on the natural law,
honed by our experiences, readings and upbringing, calling us to love and
to do good and to avoid evil.

That still, small voice enables us to take responsibility for our actions and
decisions. Our conscience is the best judge and jury of how we are leading
our lives.

When we make a good decision, the inner good feeling we get causes us to
want to do good again. It leaves an indelible mark on our conscience.

When we make a bad choice, the guilt leads us to a conversion. A
conscience willingness to change, will give us hope and mercy and the will
to make the right decisions in the future. That is what we call forming a
good conscience.

When we reflect on our lives, we can recall times when we have slipped up
and have gone against that still, small voice. Even though our conscience
knew what was right, we decided to ignore it and made a bad choice.

Each of us can recall times when we listened to our conscience, made the
right moral choice, and immediately knew that God was guiding our path.

In jail ministry, I have met many good people who have made poor
choices. They chose drugs, alcohol, sex, greed; as a result of their lack of a
well-formed conscience.

In our talks, we try to instill the desire to make better decisions and to have some successes to build a better formed moral compass.

Having trouble making the right moral decisions? Does your conscience bother you with the actions you take that go against that still, small voice in your heart?

Do you take that one more hit of heroin, one more shot of alcohol, or smoke one more joint, even though your conscience is telling you to stop?

Do you quietly and secretly seek out pornography on the internet, while your spouse and children are in the next room, with that still, small voice begging you to stop?

Are you still hiding that wedding ring when you travel for business, hoping to meet someone for casual sex, when your conscience is telling you what a beautiful family you have at home waiting for your return?

Are you trying to diet but still sneaking that afternoon candy bar and hoping it doesn't matter, when that still, small voice is telling you that you are sabotaging your health and your dieting success?

What can we do to help form a better conscience? What can we do to be more attentive to that still, small voice that moves toward good and rejects evil?

The Catechism of the Catholic Church gives us some good guidelines:

1. Realize that **the formation of conscience is a lifelong task.** We are constantly taught through practicing the virtues. We can cure our fears, selfishness, and pride. As a result we get peace of heart.
2. In the formation of conscience the **Word of God is a light for our path.** As we study the Bible, listen to homilies at Mass, get good advice from our parents, the advice and guidance of people we admire, and daily prayer, we form a stronger conscience and the ability to call on it when faced with a tough moral decision.

3. Our **conscience must be informed** and judgement enlightened. If we don't have well-formed consciences then we are vulnerable to the negative influences of others. We've got to work at it!
4. We must follow a **couple of rules**:
   1. Never do evil that good may result from it.
   2. Follow the Golden Rule—do unto others what you wish others to do to you.
   3. Do nothing to make your brother stumble.

A clear well-formed conscience is liberating. It brings us closer to our Lord. It gives us a healthy and happier life. It gives us a pure heart and a sincere faith.

In the quiet of your heart, listen; what is that still, small voice telling you?

Reflections: *Do you ever make a decision that you know is wrong but do it anyway? Do you follow your conscience? When you follow you conscience do you get a good feeling?*

The Opposite of Ego is Love

> I have been crucified with Christ. I live,
> no longer I, but Christ lives in me;
> insofar as I now live in the flesh, I live by
> faith in the Son of God who has loved
> me and given himself up for me. —
> (Galatians 2:20, NAB)

> Then he said to all, "If anyone wishes to
> come after me, he must deny himself and
> take up his cross daily and follow me.
> For whoever wishes to save his life will
> lose it, but whoever loses his life for my
> sake will save it. — (Luke 9:23-24, NAB)

We all have two voices playing in our consciousness: our ego and our sacred self. Sometimes, who we think we are and who we really are don't match. The bigger the gap between the two, the bigger our ego becomes. Our physical self (ego) gets in the way of our sacred self.

Truth is our egos can really sabotage our happiness.

Excessive ego can cause arguments, misunderstandings, prevent intimacy, and postpone reconciliation. For Christians, there is just no room for ego. Ego is pride, ignorance, and it has no feelings, no love. It's judgmental, unappreciative and relishes the failings of others.

The antidote for ego is love, humility, and peace.

Although the Bible never mentions ego, the theme of "dying to self" is a frequent theme. Dying to self becomes the model for Christians as we work to rid ourselves of the destructive effects of ego and become a more authentic version of who we really are.

How do we get in touch with our sacred self? How do we know that we are living God's plan for us? Here are some comparisons from an anonymous writer that might help us recognize our own struggle with ego:

> Ego judges others for their faults or flaws.
> Our sacred self-judges no one.
> Ego envies others for their successes.
> Our sacred self-rejoices with the success of others and
> feels their joy fully.

Ego seeks to get love and acceptance.
Our sacred self seeks to give love and acceptance.
Ego is self-centered.
Our sacred self is God and other-centered.
Ego has to get even.
Our sacred self knows to let it go.
Ego likes to fight.
Our sacred self loves to heal.
Ego blames.
Our sacred self takes responsibility.

So, how do we rid ourselves of this self-destructive ego and truly follow a more loving, humble, authentic version of ourselves? If we are to empty ourselves of ego, then we must fill the void with love, humility, and peace.

Here are some things to try:

1. **Always choose love.** Whenever we are confronted with a situation where we are being judgmental, stop! Do we really understand the person we are judging? Do we know the details of their situation? Then, why not give them the benefit of the doubt and just chose to love?

2. **Accept our own imperfections.** Often we judge others to make ourselves feel superior. We fail to come to terms with our own flaws. Accepting our own imperfections starts with not comparing ourselves with others. We should only compare ourselves with our previous self and with how far we have come on our personal journey.

3. **Quit complaining!** Life isn't perfect and neither are the people you deal with every day. Complaining gets you nowhere and simply feeds your destructive ego.

4. **Recognize God's amazing grace.** When we realize that all that we have is a gift from God and are grateful, then we are on the path toward putting our ego on hold and giving glory to God.

5. **Stay in the moment.** Ego flourishes in rehashing the past and obsessing about the future. When we have truly "died to self," we find ourselves enjoying the happiness and joy of now.

Let's try to put on Christ and lead lives that are less about our ego and more about being authentic versions of who God wants us to be.

Reflections: *Do you ever let your ego get in the way of your happiness? Do you think that arguments and misunderstandings are caused by ego? What do you do to empty yourself of ego?*

How's Your Love Life?

Beloved, let us love one another, because love is of God; everyone who loves is begotten by God and knows God. Whoever is without love does not know God, for God is love. In this way the love of God was revealed to us: God sent his only Son into the world so that we might have life through him. In this is love: not that we have loved God, but that he loved us and sent his Son as expiation for our sins. — (1 John 4:7-10, NAB)

God is love, and whoever remains in love remains in God and God in him. — (1 John 4:16, NAB)

We all have a concept of love. From the time we are very young children we have a strong sense of what love is. Ask a small child and they might tell you that love is: presents at Christmas, when my puppy licks me, when Billy shares his French fries, or when mommy kisses daddy.

As young adults, our concept of love might change. It might be reflected in the feeling we get with that new boyfriend; that first date, the first kiss, or the first Christmas together.

Later, we might define the feeling of love by our wedding day or the birth of our children; those times when life moves in slow motion as we drink in the beauty of the love we feel.

As we age, we might feel a more self-sacrificing love of taking care of a spouse with Alzheimer's, helping a loved one suffering from cancer, or growing closer while facing life's many challenges.

What is God's perspective on love?

John really seems to be the apostle of love. In his letter (1 John 4:7-5:3) John mentions love thirty-two times, God's love!

We must never forget that God loves us and gives us the perfect model of love. We love because God loved us first. God created us in His own image and likeness to be like Him; to love Him and people.

God proves His love for us by sending His only begotten son, Jesus Christ, to die for our sins. All that we have is a gift from God.

So, what are we doing to improve our love life? What are we doing to increase our love of God and neighbor? Here are a few things we can do:

1. **We love God** by our actions. Prayer and praise are a wonderful way to express our love for God, but our actions are equally important. If God is love, then we must obey Him and reach out to love others.

2. **We love ourselves** when we recognize that all that we have is a gift from God. It is difficult to love your neighbor as yourself if you don't love yourself. With all of our flaws, sins, and misgivings, we realize that we are not perfect, but instead of dwelling on the negative, we give thanks for the gifts we have been given. God loves us unconditionally and asks that we do the same for our neighbors.
3. **We love our neighbor** when we share God's love with them. We begin to treat people differently. We are less angry, more forgiving, and patient with our family and friends. When we reflect on the grace and forgiveness that God has given us, we can't help but extend that same mercy to others.

God is love and wherever there is love there is God! Is love present in your home? Then, God is there.

Do you extend your love at work, in the community, and with those you will meet today? Then, God is there.

Are you grateful for God's gifts and thank Him with praise and actions? Then, God is there.

So, how's your love life?

Reflections: *How has your perspective of love changed over the years? What do you do to emulate God's love? How's your love life?*

Grace and Gratitude

> Everything indeed is for you, so that the
> grace bestowed in abundance on more
> and more people may cause the
> thanksgiving to overflow for the glory of
> God. — (2 Corinthians 4:15, NAB)

> All good giving and every perfect gift is
> from above, coming down from the
> Father of lights, with whom there is no
> alteration or shadow caused by change.
> — (James 1:17, NAB)

Gratitude and grace—they just seem to go together. Both derived from the Latin word *gratis;* gratitude is our response to grace.

When someone does something unexpected for us, we express our thanks with gratitude, but if we have a grateful attitude, we say thank you even when things are expected.

When we dine at a restaurant, we thank the waiter for refilling our water glass and serving our meal, even though it is expected and we are paying for it. An attitude of gratitude adds to a good feeling. But, ask any server and you will find that not everyone says "thank you." Many people from our entitlement generation don't even acknowledge their server. Waitresses will tell you that these people are generally unhappy about everything.

Medical science tells us that there is an inverse relationship between gratitude and entitlement. The person with an "attitude of gratitude" has multiple health advantages over those who feel a sense of entitlement.

And, what about our relationship with God, are we grateful for all that we have? Or are we constantly unhappy because we don't possess everything we want and are jealous of others who have something we don't?

172

Our deepest sense of gratitude comes from grace. We are grateful when we realize that all that we have been given was not earned or deserved. Gratitude is our response to God's amazing grace. To live in God's grace is to be grateful. When we are grateful, we are graceful. Gratitude is a lifestyle!

However, grace comes with a price. When we are grateful for all that God has done for us, our grateful response is to be generous to others who have little. When we think of all that we have, our response must be to help others. If not, that is a cheap grace. Want to be happy? Turn your gratitude into generosity!

Here are some benefits of grace and gratefulness:

1. **Gratitude helps us cope with trauma and stress**. I am always impressed with people suffering from a terminal illness. Instead of dwelling on their illness, they express their gratitude. They really appreciate all that they have and focus their attention on what makes them feel grateful. They know that family, friends, and their faith are gifts from God, undeserved or earned, and in their gratitude our Lord showers them with grace.

2. **Gratitude builds our bonds between others and especially God**. When someone gives us a gift we are drawn to them. Our relationship grows. We want to share this feeling by blessing others, by paying it forward. The same is true for our relationship with God. The more we are grateful for what God has given us, the closer we are to Him. We are drawn to God and want to share God's blessings with others.

3. **Gratitude eliminates jealousy for others' good fortunes.** A lack of gratitude for what we have is the main cause of jealousy when a friend or relative has something we covet. A promotion at work, a new car, an honor received sets off a feeling of jealousy and causes us to concentrate on what we don't have instead of being

grateful for what we do. When we have a grateful attitude, we are happy for their good fortune.

4. **Gratitude helps us to enjoy life.** When we concentrate on what we have, especially those things that are unearned or undeserved, our attitude of gratitude will promote happiness. It will allow us to savor life, and enjoy family and friends with a deeper love and appreciation. Anger, bitterness, resentment are all replaced by happiness, joy, and grace.

5. **Gratitude makes us want to help others.** When you feel the grace that comes from being grateful, you will want to be a gift to others, serve others, and help them on their life journey. You will want them to feel the same joy that you do.

Yes, grace and gratitude just go together. The more God blesses us with His grace, the more grateful we are. The more grateful we are, the more God sends us His amazing grace. Let's make gratitude our lifestyle!

Reflections: Do you see the connection between Grace and Gratitude? What can you do to have an attitude of gratitude? What are you grateful for?

I'm All In

One body and one Spirit, as you were
also called to the one hope of your call;
one Lord, one faith, one baptism; one
God and Father of all, who is over all
and through all and in all. — (Ephesians
4:4-6, NAB)

And whatever you do, in word or in
deed, do everything in the name of the
Lord Jesus, giving thanks to God the
Father through him. — (Colossians 3:17,
NAB)

For the first time in fifty-two years, the city of Cleveland, Ohio, has a
championship. The Cleveland Cavaliers have won the NBA title and all of
Ohio has been "all in" for the team. Just like in playing poker being all in
means to invest everything, put everything on the line for one goal.

Over 1.3 million people arrived to attend the championship parade and
rally, some braving three hour waits at the bus and train lines, others
parking miles away and walking to the parade.

Our hometown hero, LeBron James is being called the "chosen one,"
Cleveland's "Savior." Main Street in Akron has been renamed "King James
Way," and pundits are referring to his leaving Cleveland for Miami and
returning as his "crucifixion" and "resurrection."

Yes, Cavs fans are all in!

Being a long time Cavaliers fan, I am thrilled. I attended game 3 of the
finals with my son who flew in from Florida, a tradition that began last
year with the loss to Golden State in game 6 of the finals, and continued
this year, only this time with a title. Hopefully, we will be together as the
Cavaliers defend their championship next June.

Wouldn't it be great if we were all in for Jesus, too?"

With the love, goodwill, camaraderie, and common purpose, just imagine if we were as passionate about our salvation through Jesus Christ. The message of Jesus—the chosen one, King of kings who truly was crucified and rose from the dead for the forgiveness of our sin—would look at lot different if more Christians were really all in for their faith.

Instead of church attendance being on the decline since 1950, churches would be overflowing, people patiently waiting in line just to get a seat.

Instead of being afraid to share our faith with others, it would become the main topic of conversation as the Cavs have become these past few weeks in Northeastern Ohio.

Instead of hiding our faith, we would be wearing tee shirts declaring our devotion as being all in for Jesus.

Just imagine it! How would our world be different? Can you imagine the love, good-will and common purpose that would exist if more Christians were all in? So what can we do to be all in for Jesus?

Celebrate His victory! Jesus's life, death, and resurrection are the greatest victory ever. Not only was it a victory over death, but He died for our sins, not just yours and mine, but everyone's.

Find Victory in the trials of others. Being a cancer survivor myself, I take great pride in celebrating with friends their victory over life's many trials. Beating cancer, finding a job after a long wait, overcoming a physical handicap and succeeding when others might question why even try, these things are worthy of us being all in in our recognition of these victories.

Give God the glory. Having the physical attributes, height and weight, and the skills to be a great athlete are often genetic. We need to thank God for these gifts. For most of us, our gifts are different. We have the skills to be great in other areas. But remember to thank God for these gifts.

It is a wonderful thing to celebrate a world championship for your town, especially when it has been over fifty years since the last title. Cleveland deserves it.

So, let me ask you: Are you all in for Jesus, too?"

Reflections: *What if people had the same enthusiasm for Our Lord? Are you all in? What does being all in mean to you?*

Chapter 5:

GOD'S GRACE IN PRAYER

What Do We Gain from Prayer?

> Amen, amen, I say to you, whatever you
> ask the Father in my name he will give
> you. — (John 16:23, NAB)

> Once a man was asked, "What did you
> gain by regularly praying to God?" The
> man replied, "Nothing…but let me tell
> you what I lost: anger, ego, greed,
> depression, insecurity, and fear of
> death." Sometimes the answer to our
> prayers is not gaining but losing; which
> ultimately is the gain. — (Anonymous)

This unattributed quote has been making its way across the internet via social media the past few weeks. Reading it, I was moved to reflect on the question, "What do we really gain from praying?"

In the quote, the man explains what he has lost through prayer, but truthfully each of the things he says he has lost are actually gains if you look to the positive.

He lost anger… but gained happiness, lost ego… but gained compassion, lost greed…but gained generosity and gratitude, lost depression…and gained joy.

He lost insecurity…but found comfort in God's word, lost fear of death….and gained everlasting life.

179

So, what do we gain from regularly praying to God? Here are some thoughts:

1. **Prayer helps our physical and psychological health.** Praying makes us feel better, reduces anxiety, and calms us in our times of need.

2. **Prayer deepens our relationship with God.** When things are going wrong, we want to tell our problems to a friend. We want someone to tell us that things will be alright; to comfort and console us. If Jesus is truly our friend, then isn't He the one best friend to offer us comfort? By going to Him, we deepen our relationship with Him and find comfort and consolation in His promise.

    > Amen, amen, I say to you, whatever you
    > ask the Father in my name he will give
    > you. — (John 16:23, NAB)

3. **Prayer helps us to draw on God's strength.** When we realize that we are helpless to solve our problems on our own and that we need God's strength to sustain us, remember Ephesians 6:10 where we are told to draw your strength from the Lord and from his mighty power. (NAB)

4. **With prayer, joy and grace are guaranteed.** God's never-ending supply of grace is waiting for us if we just ask. Prayer is the vehicle by which His grace is heaped upon us, and our depression and fears are turned to joy.

5. **With prayer, God supplies our needs and fulfills our desires.** A verse that Diane and I held close to our hearts early in our marriage was this magnificent promise from the gospel of Matthew: Again, [amen,] I say to you, if two of you agree on earth about anything for which they are to pray, it shall be granted to them by my heavenly Father. (NAB) I can't speak for others, but this promise has worked for us 100 percent of the time.

6. **With prayer, we gain wisdom.** When we are making a decision, any important decision, such as taking a new job, buying a house, picking a college to attend, or deciding on surgery, He will guide us.

> "But if any of you lacks wisdom, he
> should ask God who gives to all
> generously and ungrudgingly, and he will
> be given it." — (James 1:5, NAB)

Prayer is always positive and we profit from it whenever we pray. If we pray regularly, we not only lose *anger, ego, greed, depression, insecurity, and fear of death,* but we gain so much more.

Got a problem my friend? Why not try praying? God's grace is there for the asking.

Reflections: *Do you ever ask Jesus for help with your problems? What do you do when you realize you can't handle a situation on your own? Do you have an example of how God met your needs through prayer?*

Simon, Son of John, Do You Love Me?

> When they had finished breakfast, Jesus
> said to Simon Peter, "Simon, son of
> John, **do you love me more than
> these?**" He said to him, "Yes, Lord, you
> know that I love you." He said to him,
> "Feed my lambs." He then said to him a

second time, "Simon, son of John, do you love me?" He said to him, "Yes, Lord, you know that I love you." He said to him, "Tend my sheep." He said to him the third time, "Simon, son of John, do you love me?" Peter was distressed that he had said to him a third time, "Do you love me?" and he said to him, "Lord, you know everything; you know that I love you." [Jesus] said to him, "Feed my sheep. Amen, amen, I say to you, when you were younger, you used to dress yourself and go where you wanted; but when you grow old, you will stretch out your hands, and someone else will dress you and **lead you where you do not want to go.**" He said this signifying by what kind of death he would glorify God. And when he had said this, he said to him, "Follow me." — (John 21:15-19, NAB, Emphasis added)

In Jesus's last meeting with the apostles, He asked Peter three times, "Do you love me?" Embarrassed and humbled Peter answers him each time, "Yes, Lord, you know that I love you."

After all, Peter had denied Jesus three times and now Jesus was gently asking him to affirm his love three times.

Jesus used the Greek word "agape" the first two times that He asked the question, the deepest form of love, but Peter responded with the word "philos" a lower form, the kind of love reserved for a brother rather than a savior.

The final time Jesus asked the question, He lowered the standard for Peter by asking Peter with the word "philos." This time, Peter responded using the word "philos." His response was significant, in that Jesus was to give him the responsibility for the entire flock.

What is our response when Jesus asks us the same question, "Do you love me?" Do we respond, "Yes, Lord" as a fan or a follower, as a disciple, or just when it is convenient?

How many times have we denied Jesus, three times or three hundred times? When Jesus asked Peter if he loved Him "more that these" he probably meant the other disciples, or his boat, or fishing nets.

When He asks us this question, He might be asking if we love Him more than money, pride, possessions, an addiction, or a sin.

When we are about to break into a rant at a loved one, Jesus is asking, "Do you love me?"

When we are tempted with drugs or alcohol, Jesus is asking, "Do you love me?"

When we gossip and are about to smear the name of a neighbor, Jesus is asking us, "Do you love me?"

When a flirtation with a co-worker of the opposite sex escalates into the possibility of an affair, Jesus is asking, "Do you love me?"

He is asking if we love him with all of our heart, not only in our words but in our actions as well. Or, are we being "lead where you do not want to go."?

When we are faced with these situations, we need to pause for a moment and remember that Jesus wants us to love him "more than these," not just philos love, but agape love.

As with Peter, Jesus's question to us speaks of forgiveness and reconciliation, of those times in the past that are forgiven, if we simply can begin to answer "yes, Lord" to this basic question.

So, when Jesus asks each of us, "Do you love me?" we can answer as Peter did. We can answer, "Yes, Lord," you know that I love you."

Reflections: What is our response when Jesus asks the question of us? Are we fans or followers of Jesus? Do we answer "Yes, Lord," only when it is convenient?

Does Praying for Others Really Help?

> Therefore, confess your sins to one
> another and pray for one another, that
> you may be healed. The fervent prayer of
> a righteous person is very powerful. —
> (James 5:16, NAB)

Not a week goes by that someone doesn't ask me for prayer. It could be a relative facing surgery, a friend with a bad diagnosis, or an acquaintance asking for prayer for another.

In this age of social media, we see Facebook posts almost every day with people asking for and in need of prayer. Reading the comments on the post we see, "I'll keep you in my prayers," "My thoughts and prayers are with you," and other comments from relatives, friends, and even casual acquaintances.

It causes some people to wonder if these responses are just cliché. Some people would argue that they are just platitudes and less than sincere. But are they? Do they have any effect on the outcomes? The answer is yes!

What do these prayers mean? Research suggests that they mean more than you might imagine. A University of Toronto study indicates that people who receive these prayers are more optimistic about their situations, and that prayers promote hope, especially if they are from someone close to them.

Studies indicate that the prayers have benefit even if the recipients aren't religious themselves. Prayer works for everyone!

According to the 2006 Portraits of American Life study, two out of three Americans report having someone praying on their behalf. (Emerson, 2012) These recipients seem to be more optimistic about their future, especially when they know that non-family members are praying for them.

What makes prayer unique is the appeal to a higher power, to God, to intervene. Seventy-five percent of Americans believe that God has an interest in our health and well-being, according to a Baylor University survey. Even the unbeliever doesn't mind the support. It can't hurt, right?

Prayer does some other things as well. In addition to giving hope and optimism to the recipient, it fosters a sense of gratitude, helps us to forgive others, broadens our perspective, and gives a sense of security and comfort.

Don't be afraid to let people know that you are praying for them. Tell them. It might seem trite and cliché in this "politically correct" time that we live in, but do it anyway.

Years ago, an atheist friend of mine was facing major lifesaving surgery. The night before, as we talked on the telephone, I told him that I would pray for him during his surgery. The fact that he didn't believe in God didn't stop me. His quiet response that night was, "thank you."

The surgery was successful.

The following day, after he had returned to his hospital room following his time in recovery, he called me to tell me that things went well. It was a short upbeat conversation. As we finished our call, there was a pause in our conversation.

As my friend fought back tears, he said, "Thank you for your prayers. It meant a lot to me."

"You're welcome," I returned. "And, if I am ever in need, I hope I can count on your prayers too."

His tears were accented with a chuckle as he responded, "You sure can!"

Asking an atheist to pray for me? It can't hurt, right?

Reflections: *What do you think of the research on praying for others? When you tell someone that you will pray for them, do you? How do you respond for requests for prayer?*

Lord, Guide My Path

The human heart plans the way, but the LORD directs the steps. — (Proverbs 16:9, NAB)

> You will show me the path to life,
> abounding joy in your presence, the
> delights at your right hand forever. —
> (Psalm 16:11, NAB)

We all have times in our lives that we feel a lack of direction. No matter how much time we spend thinking about a situation, we just get more and more confused. Our anxiety levels get out of control, we are paralyzed, and we can hardly think.

It might be a problem with your marriage, starting a new job, or worse yet, losing one. It could involve a move to a new town away from family and friends, or it could be a problem with one of your children involving alcohol or drugs.

It is in these traumatic times that we realize that we can't do it alone, that we need help.

Don't fear; our Lord is here to help, if we only ask Him to guide our path. With all of the thought and planning, soul-searching and anxiety, we can still ask the Lord to direct our steps. We can put our decisions to the test, if we ask God for help.

> "You will show me the path to life,
> abounding joy in your presence, the
> delights at your right hand forever." —
> (Psalm 16:11, NAB)

In this age of technology, when we can plug an address into the GPS unit in our car and it will guide us to our destination, don't you wish there was a GPS to guide us through life's problems? There is!

Just plug in to God's eternal GPS and He will guide you in your decisions!

Psalm 37:23-24 states, "The valiant one whose steps are guided by the Lord, who will delight in his way, may stumble, but he will never fall, for the Lord holds his hand." — (NAB) (emphasis added).

Stumble as we may, isn't it great to know that we will never fail if we follow God's path, His ways? He will restore relationships, guide you in your new job, or help your search for a new one. He will help you deal with your son's addictions. When you ask the Lord to guide your path, good things happen!

How do we activate the GPS of God's direction? It's easy, just three steps.

1. **Prayer.** Simply ask the Lord for guidance. Ask for his grace and mercy, that He will show you His path and His way for your life.
2. **The Word.** Psalm 119:105 says, "Your word is a lamp for my feet, a light for my path." But reading and studying God's word, your path will be illuminated with the light of His love.
3. **Listen.** As you pray and read, ask the Holy Spirit to guide your heart. In a soft voice directly to your heart, the Holy Spirit will speak to you and help you to discern a direction for your life.

Ask the Lord to guide your path and He will show you the way. It's guaranteed. It is His promise to us. In Psalm 32:8 we read, "I will instruct you and show you the way you should walk, give you counsel with my eye upon you." (NAB)

Let's plug in to God's eternal GPS! God bless you, my friend.

Reflections: How do you activate God's GPS for your life? Have you tried this three-step approach? When was the last time you asked God for his help?

A Final Thought

Everyone I meet has a story to tell, and each is unique. These stories, passed down from generation to generation, form the fabric for understanding not only where we came from, but the hard work and struggles that were endured to get to where we are today.

Never be afraid to share your family's stories. They become the glue that connects each generation to the next.

I am so humbled to share my stories with you. I can't wait to hear yours!

Reference List

Benedict XVI. [Pontifex]. Encyclical Letter-*Spe Salvi* of the Supreme Pontiff Benedict (November 30, 2007)

Catechism of the Catholic Church [hereafter CCC], (Image Books/Doubleday, 1995), 1393

Chang, L., *Wisdom for the Soul*, (Gnosophia Publishers 1 edition,) (April 28, 2006)

Conroy, S. *Coming to Christ: Resting in His Love, Our Sunday* Visitor (October 16, 2014)

Emerson, M., and Laura J. Essenburg, *"Religious Change and Continuity in the United States: 2006-2012"* Portrait of American Life Study, http://www.thearda.com/pals/reports

Farnham, D., *Gandhi's Teachings for Troubled Times*, Amazon Digital Services LLC (September 15, 2014)

Frankl, Victor, *Man's Search for Meaning*, (Beacon Press; 4th edition, March 30, 2000)

Francis, P. [Pontifex]. *(2013, Jun 02). The world tells us to seek success, power and money; God tells us to seek humility, service and love. [Tweet]. Retrieved from https://twitter.com/pontifex/status/341135098890035200?lang=en*

Francis, P. [Pontifex]. *Dialogue between Francis and La Repubblica's founder, Eugenio Scalfari* (October 1, 2013

Francis, P. [Pontifex]. *The Christian includes; Pharisees Exclude,* Radio Vaticana, http://en.radiovaticana.va/news/2015/11/05/pope_francis_the_christian _includes;_pharisees_exclude/1184551 (May 11, 2015)

Francis, P., [Pontifex]. *Time Magazine, http://time.com/3714056/pope-francis-lent-2015-fasting/* (February 18, 2015)

Gilbert, E., *Eat, Pray, Love,* (Penguin Books, January 30, 2007)

Kesebir, P. *A Quiet Ego Quiets Death Anxiety: Humility as an Existential Anxiety Buffer,* Journal of Personality and Social Psychology 106 (4), 610-623

King, Martin Luther, *The King Center Organization,* http://www.thekingcenter.org/blog/mlk-quote-week-all-labor-uplifts-humanity-has-dignity-and-importance-and-should-be-undertaken, (April 9, 2013)

Lossky, V., Ashleigh Moorhouse and John Meyen Dorff, *The Vision of God,* St Vladimir's Seminary Press (January 1, 2013)

Millman, D., *Socrates in Way of the Peaceful Warrior: A Book that Changes Lives,* HJ Kramer; Revised edition (April 13, 2006)

Saint Rose of Lima, virgin (Ad medicum Castillo: edit L. Getino, The Patroness of America, Madrid 1928, pp. 54-55)

Theresa of Calcutta, *(Where There is Love, There is God: Her Path to a Closer Union with God and Greater Love for Others,* Image; Reprint edition (March 6, 2012)

Wooden, C. *"Lent comes 'to reawaken us,' pope says at Ash Wednesday Mass",* http://www.catholicnews.com/services/englishnews/2014/lent-comes-to-reawaken-us-pope-says-at-ash-wednesday-mass.cfm (March 5, 2014)

ACKNOWLEDGEMENTS

There are so many people to thank for their help in both the writing and publishing of *A Storyteller's Guide to a Grace-Filled Life.*

Thank you to Chuck Eberhart for the photography, graphics, the cover art, and interior design of the book. Without your help and friendship, I would be lost.

Thank you to Michelle Buckman for editing the finished book. Her editing was not only fantastic but became a writing seminar for me. Thank you to Barbara Gaskell and Jeff Flaherty, for initial rough edits

Thank you to my wife Diane for her weekly spelling and grammar checks.

A special thank you to Virginia Lieto for the encouragement throughout the process of publishing.

Thanks to Chuck Collins for his encouragement early on in my writing. That encouragement continued until he passed away.

Thank you to *Shalom Tidings Magazine,* especially Mary Job, for including my stories in their wonderful publication.

Thanks to the Catholic blogging community and the Catholic Writers Guild, especially Michael Seagriff, Elizabeth Reardon, Nancy Ward, Jeannie Ewing, Kerri Lynn Bishop, Allison Gingras, Brian Gill, Melanie Jean Juneau, David Torkington in England, Blanca Hernandez in Mexico, and Rosemarie Heirmann in Germany.

Thank you to Catholic Radio especially Living Bread Radio in Canton, Ohio, Annunciation Radio in Toledo, Ohio, Breadbox Media in Lexington, Kentucky and Gary Zimak from Spirit in the Morning in Philadelphia, Pennsylvania.